LEARNING TO LIVE WITH DOWNSIZING

LEARNING TO LIVE WITH DOWNSIZING

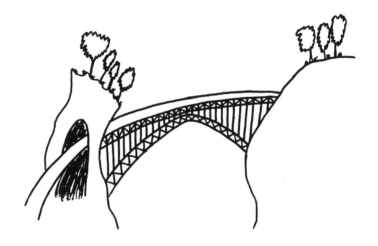

SEVEN
POWERFUL
LESSONS
FOR
BUILDING
A BRIDGE TO
TOMORROW

DEBORAH A. KING, SPHR

EMI PUBLISHING, MARIETTA, GEORGIA

ACKNOWLEDGMENTS

No accomplishment ever represents the knowledge and talents of one person alone. This creation is no exception. In my journey through life, many people have provided influence, encouragement, growth opportunities and support. So this text represents insights, research, and comments gathered from the many people with whom I have been in contact, both inside and outside of organizations that have implemented downsizing strategies.

I also have been blessed with the love and emotional support of my husband, Stephen, who never ceased believing that this book would be born. My sister, Dr. Terri Gabrielson, was always ready to refill my spirit with hope and reignite my dedication to the project. And my dear writer friends in WW:OR never failed to boost my confidence and creativity.

There also are many other colleagues, friends, family and clients who have cheered me on as the story in my mind became the story you are about to read. I do not include their names, as there are many and I worry I would inadvertently leave key contributors off the list. I trust they know who they are and will accept a simple "thank you" as an expression of my gratitude and appreciation.

Marietta, Georgia
Deborah A. King
October 1996

CONTENTS

PREFACE

Learning To Live With Downsizing focuses on the impact the strategy of downsizing has on the company, its employees and the community. The phenomenon of Survivor Syndrome is examined in search of more appropriate responses, by management and each individual, for redefining the new employment relationship. The Integrated Downsizing Approach (IDA) is discussed as an alternative downsizing strategy, one that considers the needs of the business, those employees leaving the organization, those remaining, and the community that supports and monitors the citizenship role of the firm.

History suggests American businesses, regardless of industry or size, always have been somewhat sensitive to competition, cost control and technology. But global events over the past 10 years have rendered urgent the need to search for new business strategies to define future success.

Those who have seen or felt Survivor Syndrome understand why it affects the performance of the organization in transition. Employees become paralyzed by fear: fear of the unknown, fear of losing their jobs, fear of looking for another job, fear of the skill level required by a high-tech world, fear of going back to school, fear of family reaction, fear of meeting financial obligations, and on and on.

Understanding Survivor Syndrome helps managers develop strategies to help employees build resistance to it. It also helps individuals realize the need to redefine themselves and their past perceptions of the employment relationship — and, it is hoped, realize that resiliency and flexibility are critical characteristics required to meet the changing world head-on.

As organizations chart their courses to the future, they are exploring ways to replace the old psychological contract - that is, the implied agreement that suggests the employer will keep the employee in service until retirement or resignation. Experiments with options and interventions are beginning, including in-house career development centers, change-management workshops, flexible work hours, greater decision-making authority, support for continuous training and telecommuting.

We know that some type of relationship must exist between the employer and employee. We also know that it is unhealthy to offer a false sense of job security. The new relationship that develops after downsizing must evolve from the culture of the company in transition and must be modeled, encouraged and supported from the top. However, it also must recognize that the emotions and attitudes of surviving employees will be inclined toward self-survival rather than the good of the company. A common ground must be found between the two parties that accommodates the company's objectives even as it gives employees the opportunity to develop and remain employable — no matter what happens to the company in the future.

This Book's Purpose and Audience

Survivor Syndrome is a sickness that influences the attitudes, feelings and behaviors of all employees — regardless of their position — when they are confronted with the reality that not only have they lost their job security, they also could lose their jobs.

Learning To Live With Downsizing strives to offer practical information about this sickness, as well as lessons for dealing with it. To be sure, reality can be depressing. That's why

Learning To Live With Downsizing was developed as a business novel, a sort of corporate fable. The language of the text is meant to be conversational and unacademic, even as the message educates and provides a model of how interventions may be constructed to assist the individual, as well as the team, with confronting feelings, emotions and fears. Only then can an action plan be implemented that makes it possible to build a bridge from today to tomorrow.

Downsizing is not a fad. Nor is there much of a chance that it will go away. The book is intended to be used as a introduction for organizations preparing to travel the road of downsizing. It also is an invaluable pretraining assignment for organizations that already have downsized and are now providing the assistance employees need to move beyond Survivor Syndrome. After all, only after the disease is conquered can its survivors re-energize and recommit to the company's new vision and performance goals.

PART ONE

THE JOURNEY

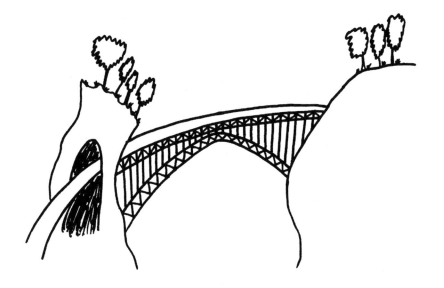

AN ADVENTURE NOT TO
BE FORGOTTEN

Once upon a time, in a place very, very far away, there existed a village that was bustling with creative, happy and productive people....

☆ ☆ ☆ ☆

The air, still and heavy under a thick blanket of fog, was typical of a rainy Spring morning in Atlanta. Stephanie sat in her office, twisting a lock of strawberry blonde hair and contemplating working on her computer. It was unusual for her to be in her home-based office on a Saturday, a day she normally reserved for gardening gloves, dungarees and pruning shears. Gazing through the window at the April showers and leaden sky, she found herself wishing the weather forecast was more optimistic so she could begin her spring planting in those lovely garden beds of hers. But, alas, it was not to be.

With a forecast that was not going to cooperate with Plan A, gardening, Stephanie decided to tackle Plan B: surfing the Internet. Reconciling herself to the fact that gardening would have to wait for another day, she turned her attention to cyberspace (wherever *that* was, she smiled to herself) and to her computer training.

Stephanie's interests hadn't always included gardening, let alone the Internet. As a human resource executive in a large communications company, there was little time for anything other than work, work and more work. Her heretofore undiscovered fondness for gardening actually had been born of advice from her doctor, who had sternly informed her that if she couldn't learn healthy ways to manage her stress, she would face serious consequences. Stephanie remembered that the words "heart attack" were used. (How could she forget? she thought. The words still ring in my ears!) But he got her attention, and she discovered a new hobby.

Of course, Mother Nature didn't always cooperate. That's when Stephanie spent time in her office, formerly a second bedroom, permitting her fingers to skip over the keyboard and her hand to guide her mouse as it swiped at menu-driven commands. When prompted, she typed in 'ROSEBUD' and listened as the computer dialed up the local Internet connection. She smiled to herself, envisioning an old-fashioned rotary phone floating weightless in space, seeking in vain a phone-jack friend and ringing, ringing — pleading "answer me!" to the stars and asteroids whizzing by. She knew that her computer was dialing the Netcom connection in Atlanta, but that reality was dull. It was much more fun to picture the phone being answered by someone in outer space. Imagination, she decided, has no boundaries.

4

Stephanie assigned to herself the status "novice" when it came to navigating the Internet. Only recently had she begun to visit cyberspace. Everything she knew (and that was just the basics), she had taught herself. She considered herself still very much a learner and explorer and was amazed by the technology that permitted her to dash from here to there and all over the universe, as well, exploring new topics and "meeting" new people.

A small click announced a successful connection to the server had been made and Stephanie began tapping at the keyboard again, scrolling through the list of available Web sites. She paused briefly to perform the head-roll exercise recommended as a stay against neck tension, and then resumed her investigation of the available Websites. As she glanced through her options, she was curious about one that seemed to jump out at her: **Virtual Cove**. With a quick click of her mouse, she was off on an adventure she would never forget.

☆ ☆ ☆ ☆

The script that rolled out across her screen was a strange hybrid of an old Roman font adorned with New Age swirls and scrolls. "Virtual Cove," Stephanie murmured to herself. The Web page was hard to miss. It seemed real enough - indeed, as it flashed neon-type invitations to explore the future as it would apply to travel, entertainment, business opportunities and food. But, the backdrop of the page was rather odd, afloat with crisp colors and strange shapes that had Stephanie imagining something of a cross between what life would be like on Mars and living as a comic-book caricature. And what did that icon represent that kept appearing and disappearing into the shadow, as though it wanted to catch her attention and lure her into the depths of the screen?.

As she studied the page, it seemed to vibrate and glow. Stephanie stared, sensing a challenge. "That's silly," she frowned. "It's just words, for Pete's sake!" Other than a vividly wild web page, and fonts that suggested someone had played fast and loose with the graphics, there was nothing that should have struck her as unusual about it. Yet she sensed that there was more, that this was a facade. She felt a presence, though she heard nothing. It was a sort of vibration, a feeling that made it hard for her to swallow. As she considered the weirdness of this site, she decided there was no harm in exploring and clicked her mouse on the word "welcome."

For some reason, the image of Alice disappearing down the hole after the White Rabbit leapt into her mind. The image should have amused her. It didn't.

It happened then. Her only warning was that she felt suddenly overpowered by an unseen presence pulling at her through her monitor. Stephanie's heart jumped into her throat when the invisible creature began tugging, pulling her forward. She was frozen, her mind a blur of panic, and only after she felt herself being sucked into a great, dark vacuum was she able to scream.

☆ ☆ ☆ ☆

What seemed like an eternity was at once too quick to measure. Stephanie felt herself being tossed against the walls of a raging funnel cloud that had seized her. Unwilling to relinquish its newfound treasure, it held her in its furious grasp and tossed her petite frame about until she thought she would pass out, every bone broken. It was as though she was trapped in a blender that raged out of control, and she was unable to free herself.

6

But she felt no pain. Nothing was broken. When an updraft thrust her against the funnel's walls and pinned her there, her panic at being no more substantial than a rag doll was replaced by an odd exhilaration at her own defiance of gravity. Finally, mercifully, she was enfolded in a sense of absolute peace, and the world went dark.

When she awoke, Stephanie was leaning against a light pole planted on the corner of what appeared to be a main street in an office park. The lawns were carefully landscaped and the trees were in full, glorious bloom, heralding the arrival of Spring. What would have been a pastoral scene was disturbed by odd architectural configurations (office buildings? she wondered) that loomed ominously. Stephanie rubbed her eyes and gazed up at the spires that topped assorted domes and bubbles. Bizarre, but not threatening, she decided.

Somehow, the environment, though conspicuously foreign, was at once familiar, despite air that was still and strange. She assumed this was some type of business district, but was without clue as to where it was on the map or how she happened to be there.

Confusion had replaced panic. That is, until a man suddenly and without warning jumped out of the alley to her right. He stumbled a little as he fell forward, regained his balance and charged, waving his arms above his head and screaming words she could not understand. Stephanie, terrified, turned and ran, expecting anything from gun shots to worse.

Her feet pounded the pavement beneath her and buildings streaked by. No one came to her rescue — the streets were eerily empty, though she had been so sure she could feel the presence of people inside the weird-looking buildings. How could they ignore this commotion outside? What kind of place was this? Later, she would remember it and it would remind her of a plot line for TV's *Twilight Zone*.

7

Stephanie charged over landscaped lawns, dodging shrubbery and hydrants and whatever else was in her way. She ran for what seemed a lifetime. Finally, when she was about to cave in to exhaustion, she heard her attacker's shouts. He had gained enough on her to call out and be heard. Not good, she thought.

"Stop! I give up. Come back!"

Stephanie, breathing hard and face flushed, slowed a little to glance back over her shoulder. He was there, all right, but apparently, he was no more an exercise enthusiast than she was. He had collapsed on the park bench and didn't look like he was going anywhere soon.

"I'm sorry I scared you," he shouted.

Hoping for a momentary truce, Stephanie stopped, bent double at the waist and grabbed her ankles, her breath coming in short, sharp gasps. Her legs felt as though they were made of rubber. Weak and barely able to breath, she felt she had just enough energy left to straighten up and limp over to a circular tower painted in a spiral of yellow and green, a surreal sort of silo.

No sooner had she reached it than she collapsed against it, drained. Please let this dream be over, she thought. Leaning with her back against the outside wall, she closed her eyes and pressed her palms against the hard, cold stone.

Wait. Something's weird, she thought. What was it?

Running her palms over the surface of the outside wall, she realized that she could actually *feel* the building. Stephanie had been hoping, believing even, that what was happening was not real, that she was asleep and would wake to again find herself at her computer. But in all the hours of her life that she had spent in slumber, she had never actually *felt* anything in a dream. Not as vividly as she was feeling cold hard stone.

She took a deep breath and inhaled the scent of flowers and trees. Birds chirped and in the distance, she heard a shrill, hollow echo somewhere up above. Scanning the vast milky sky, her eyes caught sight of billowing twin trails streaming behind a silver speck. A plane or space ship? She could see it and she could hear it. Most definitely this was not a dream.

"Please! Come back. I promise I won't hurt you or scare you again."

Stephanie had almost forgotten about him. Looking back at the bench where he had parked himself, she saw that he was still there. He appeared not to be going anywhere fast — clearly, he was too exhausted to resume the chase. Now that she had confirmed that she could outrun him, she decided to take a chance. She wasn't sure what would happen, but she had to at least find out where she was, who this man was and why he was chasing her.

Wiping the perspiration from her forehead, she took a deep breath and turned a very purposeful stride toward him. As matter-of-fact confident as she hoped she appeared, she prayed he wouldn't harm her. Maybe, if she was really lucky, he would even help her find her way home.

☆ ☆ ☆ ☆

His name was Harry Tipwell. When she demanded to know what his profession was and what, if anything, it had to do with scaring her half to death, he revealed he was Chief (as he put it) of Virtual Travel Corporation and Ambassador of Virtual Cove. He certainly looked every bit the part: As he spoke, Stephanie assessed what he was wearing — khaki-colored Chinos, a navy blue blazer and a starched white shirt opened at the neck — and determined it was the costume of many professional men she had encountered in Atlanta.

9

"Again," he was saying, "let me apologize. I'm so sorry if I scared you. And again, welcome"— this, as he offered his hand. Stephanie hesitated before she took it, though something told her that it would be okay. His was not the face of a terrorist or a sociopath.

"Why were you chasing me?" she demanded, voice curt. "Is this the way you welcome people to your town?"

"Uh, no. What I was..."

"Where am I?"

"Well, like I said, this is Virtual..."

"So how did I get here?"

"Probably, you were sur..."

"And why were you chasing me like that?" she suddenly screamed.

Harry had expected it. He knew she was going to be upset — he had seen it before. Motioning to Stephanie to take a seat next to him on the bench, he began, "I know this is very confusing to you. Let me guess: You were surfing on the Web when you selected 'Virtual Cove' as your Web site connection. Am I right?"

"Yeah," Stephanie breathed. "How did you know?"

"Well..." he began, and stopped. "I'm sorry, but I didn't catch your name."

"Stephanie. Stephanie Cromby."

"You see, Stephanie," he continued, "this has happened before. We've been trying to get our site off the Internet, but there seems to be some crossed communication waves and satellite linkages that have us trapped in a frequency lock. Whatever it is, it won't allow us to cancel the site, and every now and then a 'surfer' drops in. But I must confess that usually, these surfers are kids about 13 or so. They love virtual reality games and think a visit to our site is just another game.

"Well, it's not a place to play games! And I'm getting pretty damn tired of having to chase kids out of town."

Stephanie could see and hear his frustration, but she was puzzled. "If you don't want visitors in Virtual Cove, why have a Web site?" she ventured, almost timid. "And anyway, I thought one visited Web sites through a computer. Since when can you actually GO there?"

Harry was quiet for a moment. "That's what makes our site so special," he finally replied.

By now, both Stephanie and Harry had caught their breath and were a little more relaxed. She had abandoned the notion that Harry, with his round, expressive face that reminded her of a playful rubber mask, was capable of committing anything approaching harm. He, meanwhile, had determined that as much as she had acted like she wanted to a moment ago, she probably wasn't going to clobber him.

Harry gripped the edge of the bench, using it as leverage to ease up from a sitting position and wincing a little as he did so. Slowly, he straightened and stood, looking down at her. "I think to explain what is going on, Stephanie, I really need to go back to the beginning. Let's walk through the park and talk. There's a place near here where we can get something to drink."

VIRTUAL COVE'S STORY

"Let me start at the beginning," Harry said, as they selected a spot at a picnic table next to a gurgling creek. "I came to Virtual Cove about 15 years ago." A grin stretched across the tanned rubber mask, still flushed from the chase. "In fact, I arrived in a similar fashion as yourself.

"You see, I was a lieutenant in the Army, assigned to lead a team of computer experts on a Superhighway project. Twenty years ago, we were just starting to get a handle on what resources could be harnessed to design a huge linkage of data. Of course, our first goal was to focus on national security issues. But to those of us with interest and vision, applications for this technology on the civilian side also were apparent.

"One afternoon, I was on leave after working nonstop for a full two weeks. Our project, which was highly confidential, was focused on developing the technology to transport objects, from coffee cups to tanks, from one location to another. The military saw a lot of applications for this 'transport technology' to earth maneuvers as well as outerspace missions. I liked what I was doing, but I was personally more interested in transporting people from one spot to another. I had gone so far as to rig up this really crude machine in my apartment and was experimenting with expanding the technology in my free time, when *it* happened. One afternoon, using my special machine, I locked in on a destination. To my surprise and delight, seconds later I found myself in Virtual Cove."

Stephanie studied his pleasant face and watched as the animated mask twisted itself into an expression of excitement

"Wow!" he suddenly exclaimed, jumping up from the table. "I felt like I hit the jackpot!

"Back then, this was a bustling center for creative cyber-space entrepreneurs from all over the universe," he went on, sinking back into his seat. "Everywhere you went, you met people with creative ideas, people willing to take a chance on something new in an effort to contribute to the advancement of technology. Some of them were even working on the Superhighway. Workers in organizations were not only moti-vated, they were actually passionate about their work.

"After a few days of the best kind of virtual reality game I could ever imagine, I decided I didn't want to go back. I found a way to have my cake and eat it too. I could still do the work I was interested in, but do it from a totally new living envi-ronment. So I stayed," he sighed.

"As you will see, there are many different types of people here in Virtual Cove, so they are very accepting of people from other places. But some things have changed, and I miss those things. People here seemed to be interested in good ideas, no matter where you came from. Now," Harry paused, studying Stephanie's face. "Now that's changed."

"'Changed'?" Stephanie asked.

☆ ☆ ☆ ☆

The warm Spring sun, which had emerged to burn the haze from the sky, was settling into the tops of the trees for the afternoon. Harry looked at Stephanie, his face dappled by light filtered through leaves. "It's a sad story," he finally replied.

"Go ahead," she urged.

"Well. Okay. What happened was this: Because companies here were doing so well financially, they were able to offer great benefits and wages to their employees, and everyone got along as one big family. I can remember having terrific summer picnics, right here at this park. The company would sponsor baseball games, pitting one department against another, and there was always a lot of delicious food. The workers who did arts and crafts would set up a tent to hawk their wares — you wouldn't believe the variety of arts that were brought here from the different cultures these people came from. Always, there were clowns, and storytellers, and the latest in virtual games. There were even ice-cream eating contests for the kids. It was great fun and a wonderful time.

14

"But those were different times. We really felt secure with our jobs and couldn't imagine the trouble we were setting ourselves up for as we cultivated what turned out to be a false sense of hope and security. We never thought about leaving our companies, or this site. We saw ourselves working hard at what we believed in even as we were rewarded with good wages, benefits, training, promotions and annual raises. We knew we would receive future rewards — what we used to call 'retirement' back on Earth. Most likely a party would be given in our honor, at which our contributions would be vigorously praised. We fondly imagined that the lazy days of our retirement would have us periodically stopping back to visit with the new workers and check on how they were doing without us.

"And as funny as it appears now, we actually felt the company encouraged the retired to do this, just to sort of maintain the family connections."

As Harry spoke, Stephanie observed a marked change in his demeanor. He slumped in his seat. He dropped his head.

The wonderful rubber mask had taken on a worried look, as though he were about to disclose something that should be of great concern.

"What is it?" she asked, curious.

☆ ☆ ☆ ☆

"Things began to change," he mumbled. "It was subtle at first, but it grew like a virus."

"But what happened?" Stephanie implored, leaning closer. "It sounds like this was a thriving city. What could change that?"

Harry looked wistful. Glancing down at his hands, fingers working, he replied, "The Internet. That's what happened. The very thing we were working so hard to build ruined us. We were too busy and too full of our success to see it coming. And now we're stuck and can't seem to move forward."

Now Stephanie was even more curious. "How did the Internet create a problem?"

Harry sighed. "As I told you, many companies were doing well. Some of them made a fortune supplying the world with software, knowledge, and creative ideas about how the Internet would unite us in ways we never dreamt of," he said. "These organizations were very involved with cutting-edge ideas about how to put all kinds of information at our fingertips — communication without wires, travel without planes, entertainment opportunities so futuristic that Hollywood hadn't thought of them yet. The kinds of things we worked on would change the way we lived and worked forever, no matter what planet or corner of cyberspace we occupied.

"What our business community didn't count on was the competition that would come from other business communities, in other galaxies. We underestimated how the changing technology, even some that we were promoting, would affect our own industry. We didn't foresee the impact of what you on earth call 'globalization,' how the shift of jobs within the universe would impair our ability to compete.

"Slowly," he continued, "we saw our market share dwindle and our profit margin shrink. By this time, I had my own firm and was responsible for the lives and careers of more than 3,000 workers. We weren't sure what was happening, but we knew we wanted to proceed cautiously and not overreact. We were reluctant to take action. We were sure this was just a blip on the cosmic screen and that our business volume would again be restored to previous levels."

Harry gazed into the creek, watching but not really seeing water that tumbled over stones and threaded its way among cattails standing like sentinels in the overgrowth. "I guess, looking back on it, we were in some kind of denial," he mused. "We didn't want to admit that our business strategies may not have been as visionary as they should have been. We didn't want to face the fact that we had created a culture in which all of our workers now relied on us to dictate their every move. Some of us had corporate cultures that encouraged workers to think outside the box, but even then, we selfishly discouraged the transference of this thinking to themselves, their careers and their families. We orchestrated their compensation and recognition to get them to buy into *our* values and the behaviors we were looking for. We unwittingly developed strategies that gradually robbed them of the values they personally cherished.

"I don't know," he said, sounding exhausted, "perhaps we couldn't admit failure. We just denied there was a problem and tried to go on with business as usual. We didn't make any shifts in strategies. We didn't communicate with our employees. We continued to market the same way, we continued to hire more employees, we didn't evaluate different market segments, or determine whether we should stay in the ones we were already in. Eventually, we would pay for this with our culture, employee trust and customer satisfaction.

"Then, without much warning, we saw our strategies — those which up until now had positioned us to be the front-runner, the one on the leading edge — turn sour. Our financial success was eroding. With loss of market, and competitors looming on the horizon, we found ourselves overstaffed and with greater expenses than we could afford. In a frantic attempt to compensate for our lack of vision, we made some quick decisions that ultimately made things worse.

17

"For some reason, the decision to downsize did not play out the way we thought it would. We haven't been able to achieve our performance and profitability goals. In fact, our competitiveness and efficiency is lower now than it was *before* the downsizing."

Harry glanced at the watch that he had pulled from his shirt pocket. It was on a chain, like an old-fashioned pocket watch, but Stephanie saw the face was anything but. The hour hand was a bright laser-type light that blinked while the minute hand was created by the mist of a space ship traveling around the dial.

He had been speaking for more than two hours. "Would you like to grab lunch?" he asked.

The pair walked through the park toward Harry's office, and Stephanie confessed that she was worried about getting home. I can help you with that, he assured her. I know how. "By tonight, you'll be back in your home without a problem," he said smiling.

Stephanie was relieved, and marveled that she actually trusted this stranger who just a short time ago had terrified her. In fact, if she was really honest, she was beginning to enjoy herself.

☆ ☆ ☆ ☆

As they drew closer to the headquarters for Harry's company, Stephanie noticed a giant advertisement that hung, magically suspended from the sky.

"The only card you need — Virtual Travel Card," it read.

When they entered the lobby, Stephanie stopped dead in her tracks and gasped at what could only be the set of a sci-fi movie. Several columns rendered in assorted geometric shapes and randomly placed around an expanse of room appeared to support nothing. The walls, dressed up in wild shades of pink and orange, glittered as though painted with moon dust. The sun cast its light through large windows situated in the ceiling — skylights, but tinged with colors that reminded Stephanie of butter mints. She was awestruck, a first-time-tourist to the big city.

Harry gave her a minute to take it all in before he spoke. "The reason I'm certain you'll safely return to your home in Atlanta is because my company was the first to develop the technology that allows people to *really* explore virtual reality. With our specially coated travel card and software, you can relive situations not unlike those in your movie *Back To The Future*, but with considerably less hassle."

They stopped at the security desk to pick up a visitor's badge for Stephanie. As she waited, she could not help but notice the employees stationed there. Two women, seated at a spherical silver work station that reminded Stephanie of a UFO, seemed anything but happy, friendly or even particularly interested in their work. Their motions were automatic, almost robotic; their voices, when they spoke at all, were listless monotones. Not that Stephanie had occasion to hear much more than "Sign the register, please." Nobody asked where she was from, or even greeted her. They seemed to just be biding their time.

Harry ushered Stephanie into the cafeteria where, as she would have expected, the layout and design mirrored that of the lobby. The irony of a fun, creative work environment utilized by low-spirited, apathetic employees was not lost on her — something was seriously wrong.

Stephanie was hungry. The wonderful aroma of various foods almost was evidence enough that this cafeteria fare was fresh and prepared on the premises, but she wasn't going to bet on it — it was too high-tech to be believable. She and Harry placed their orders with roving robots that shuffled to and from the kitchen, and her eyes wandered the room, taking in yet more lifeless employees sitting at flat chrome tables.

Settling in at a table in the corner and waiting for Harry, who had asked permission to check his messages, she overheard a disturbing conversation taking place. It was coming from the direction of the next table, where two women — one younger, one graying and matronly — and a young man, probably in his mid-thirties, sat.

"It's only noon," the younger woman complained. "I just dread coming in here, and once I'm here, it seems like time just stops and I'll never end my shift."

"Did you see the latest memo?" interjected the man. "They want us to get involved with the new 'create-a-product' campaign. Yeah, like I'd step up and offer my ideas about a new product. That way, if they didn't like it, they could put my name on the list for the next round of layoffs. Why would anyone want to take the risk?"

"Speaking of layoffs," chirped the matron, "have you heard the latest from the vine? They say there's been a lot of activity up on the top floor — lots of closed doors, folks not seeing their managers in days — and they're saying another round of layoffs is coming as early as next month.

"I've been lucky, if you can say that, to have survived the five cuts we've already been through," she continued. "I'm scared I won't survive this round, though." Her voice was tearful. "I've no idea how I'll make ends meet if I have to leave. I've been here 15 years and I dread looking for a new job. Who's going to want someone my age? I'm worried I might lose my home, and here my kid is studying at the university. How will I manage that expense? Not to mention that I'll lose my medical coverage and benefits."

☆ ☆ ☆ ☆

As Stephanie awaited Harry's return, she again surveyed the room. Clearly, what was happening to Virtual Travel was very similar to, if not the same as, what had happened to her company in Atlanta. She had seen the same unmotivated behavior. She had heard the same kind of remarks underscored by fear.

The dilemma intrigued her. It also gave her leverage. What if she and Harry could swap information about organization development in the aftermath of downsizing? In exchange for what she knew and would share, he would be sure to make good on his promise to return her to her home.

When Harry finally arrived, he was visibly upset. One of his workers at a plant outside of town had to be restrained by armed security officers after he arrived at work, armed with a laser gun. Harry had never had to deal with a situation like this. What, if anything, should he do about the stress and anxiety his employees were feeling? He pondered the situation aloud.

"Why aren't these workers doing something to prepare themselves for the future instead of resisting the inevitable?" he asked. Then, not waiting for a reply: "Why can't they accept that things are never going to be the same as they were before? What am I supposed to do — meet with every single employee and hold his or her hand while each charts a course for the new culture?"

Stephanie didn't respond. She sat and listened while Harry voiced frustrations that seemed to have been suppressed for some time. "I don't know what's come over me," he concluded helplessly.

"That's okay," she assured him. "It sounds like you needed to get all that out in the open."

A pause. And then: "Now that it's out, can I ask you a few questions?"

☆ ☆ ☆ ☆

AGREEING TO MEET THE CHIEFS

About five years ago, executives at Stephanie's company announced the decision to cut the work force. She'd never forget that day, when every worker was summoned to massive meeting places located throughout the Southern territory. Nor would she forget Albert Thompson, company president and CEO, who stood behind the podium, uneasily shifting his weight from one foot to the other as he waited for the meeting to begin. Stephanie had heard rumors, but after witnessing the behavior of a leader who usually was at ease in front of crowds, she began to dread the worst.

He began by reminding his audience what a great company they worked for. Still, times were changing, and... . By the time he got to the real issue, the numbers were staggering: The work force would be cut by 20 percent, or about 3,000 workers. It was well beyond what Stephanie had imagined.

Life, she decided, had not been the same since. The work force had been pared again after that; later, another series of cuts were made. After the first two downsizings, Stephanie felt unprepared to adequately fulfill her role as human resources director. She observed, and felt, the pain of those who had been asked to leave, and the confusion and guilt of those chosen to stay. Not that she was alone in her feelings of inadequacy — many managers confided that they distrusted their ability to handle their own emotions about the changes, let alone those of their workers.

Stephanie had plenty of useful information and knowledge gathered from her college days and human behavior classes. But she suspected there was more she needed to know in order to completely understand what she was witnessing. For months she read as much as she could about downsizing and an associated sickness called "Survivor Syndrome." She had contacted other companies at which similar downsizing strategies were being adopted to inquire about the attitudes and behaviors they were experiencing with their work force. She believed she was now at the stage where, having collected data, she could implement interventions to help address and correct negative, unproductive and ultimately destructive attitudes, beliefs and behaviors being demonstrated by many company employees.

She had gathered information and had implemented some practices to help the employees deal with changing cultures and expectations. But as she sat listening to Harry and observing Virtual Cove, she wondered if this was a chance — a unique one, to say the least — to further explore the impact of downsizing.

☆ ☆ ☆ ☆

"Have you ever heard of a sickness called Survivor Syndrome?" she asked. Harry, puzzled, frowned and shook his head. "Well," she continued, "Survivor Syndrome is a term used to describe the attitudes, emotions and behaviors exhibited by employees who survive in a company after a significant layoff. The reason I have heard about it is my company in Atlanta also has been struggling with many of the issues you have been speaking about. In fact, if we were sitting in Atlanta, I would have wondered whether you were talking about my firm.

"From what I've learned, not all employees suffer from all the symptoms. But research indicates they *all* experience *some* symptoms to a degree. The longer the disease is left to fester without attention, the more extensive the symptoms can get. In fact, some employees can be so traumatized by downsizing that it's almost impossible for them to be effective on their job, no matter how much skill and knowledge they have, and regardless of their past performance. The sickness becomes paralyzing.

"But being armed with that knowledge isn't enough. Survivor Syndrome is difficult to manage. It takes a lot of courage to face the reality of what is happening and to help yourself, much less help your co-workers."

This time it was Harry's turn to be intrigued. "If what you say is true, and I have certainly seen some of this paralyzing behavior, I need to learn more about Survivor Syndrome," he said. "Tell me something, Stephanie. Have you experienced it at your company?"

☆ ☆ ☆ ☆

24

Stephanie began by telling Harry about her role. She had held the position of human resources director for six years and had, almost since starting, been busy gaining exposure to downsizing-related issues.

Her company also had suffered from rapid technological advancement, governmental regulation and the impact of the global market. As a result, her communications firm had re-engineered, restructured, rightsized — "you name it, we did it," she said, watching Harry furiously scribble notes on what appeared to be a computerized tablet. She couldn't help but notice that the pen he used glowed at the tip, where normally the ball point would be located. Not wanting to be rude, she went on, pretending to be unfazed. "Sometimes I think our CEO just didn't wanted to show up at a meeting with his CEO peers and have to admit he hadn't at least tried some of these new methods they were all talking about.

"Seriously, it got so bad that, for awhile, it was like management by trend-of-the-week. And that's when I learned about Survivor Syndrome. I had to! Our survival as a company depended on it."

Harry, mind racing, wondered if he could tap into Stephanie's knowledge before she returned to Earth. "I have so much to ask you," he began. "Is there any way you would consent to staying in Virtual Cove for a few days? Perhaps you can take some vacation?"

Stephanie was surprised by the request. Perhaps she was becoming more relaxed about being in this new place, but she also was extremely interested in securing a safe trip home — the sooner the better. True, she was amazed by the similarities between her company and Virtual Travel. She was interested in learning more about their situation and, she had to admit, eager to share what she had learned. She hesitated as she looked at Harry's hopeful face. She knew this would be a good experience for him, and she believed she'd learn something new that would benefit her work teams back on Earth.

But what about getting back home?

"Are you *sure* there's not going to be a problem getting me home?" she asked, feeling a little foolish.

Harry shook his head. "Stephanie, I promise you, the trip back will be quick and gentle, and we can do it at any moment. Please consider staying a little longer. I think it would be so helpful to share what we have experienced and to learn from you, as well."

Stephanie considered his proposal. "Okay," she finally consented, surprising herself. "I'll stay this afternoon, but tonight I'm going home."

Harry was delighted. Stephanie would meet with other Chiefs in the business community of Virtual Cove. He wasted little time relaying the news to them via an electronic mail system similar to Stephanie's e-mail back on Earth. Then, as Chiefs from across the cyberspace office park returned RSVPs, Harry turned his attention to making meeting arrangements and Stephanie began preparing her notes.

It's odd, she thought, but I'm having fun. She was eager to meet the Chiefs and learn about their own experiences. She also was looking forward to a chance to meet with their workers, and if time allowed, take a first-hand look at several of their operations. As Stephanie completed her notes and glanced at her outline, she felt energized. Somehow, she knew she'd be learning as much as she taught.

OUTLINE

The Lessons

1 Survivor Syndrome: A Sickness that Affects the 4 Ps: Profitability, Productivity, Performance and Personal Health

2 Integrating the Needs of Business, Employees and Community

3 Coaching Yourself and Others

4 What's Driving Downsizing Strategy

5 Minimizing the Effects of Negative Emotions and Behaviors

6 Benefiting from the Changing Employment Relationship

7 Building Personal Independence and Employability

Yes, that should do it, she thought, sitting back in her chair and looking out the window at the cartoon-like city. Somehow she felt it had welcomed her, though that welcome had been extended in a most unusual way.

PART TWO

THE LESSONS

LESSON ONE

Survivor Syndrome: A Sickness that Affects the
4 Ps: Profitability, Productivity, Performance
and Personal Health

One of Virtual Cove's greatest and (in Stephanie's mind) most redeeming qualities was time's ability to pass as fast or as slow as one wanted it to. So it really seemed like a matter of minutes before the men and women Harry had contacted began to assemble in the huge auditorium at the Virtual Travel headquarters.

As with the other rooms Stephanie had been in, the auditorium could only be described as high sci-fi. Not only did it boast excessively unusual architecture, it featured a variety of incredible technological advancements to facilitate Stephanie's presentation.

There was, for example, a laser tablet. Somehow, the words Stephanie penned on it (using an oversized, inkless pen that glowed at its tip) appeared on the wall screen that hung at the front of the room. All she had to do was push a button to make it happen. Another marvel, known as a "laser interpreter," permitted her to speak into a beeper-sized recorder. As with the tablet, the words she spoke surfaced on the screen.

The wall screen. Even that seemingly innocuous piece of equipment was bizarre, she thought. As with Virtual Travel's futuristic billboard, the wall screen was mysteriously suspended mid-air, with nary a hook, nail or wire to be seen.

Harry told Stephanie that all the Chiefs in attendance were from operations that had already downsized or where seriously considering doing so. All were interested in learning about the effects of downsizing and would appreciate and lessons that Stephanie could pass on from her experiences on Earth.

After everyone had settled at their tables and conversation had subsided, Harry introduced her to a group of about 20 executives. He made a point of reciting the background information she had provided about her profession and experience, and explained the events leading up to her unexpected arrival in Virtual Cove.

It was Stephanie's turn to take the floor. As the platform stage was not very high, she was situated at a good vantage point from which to examine the faces and body language of her audience. What she saw did not surprise her — it was not unlike her own company, where burnout, stress and low energy levels were betrayed by lifelessness and lethargy. They were people embattled by uncertain futures and the struggle to manage their companies' survival. Walking across the stage, she stationed herself behind the podium and looked out at the attendees.

Stephanie situated herself behind the podium. Considering it, she decided it resembled a comic-book rocket. I wonder what I look like behind this thing, she thought, amused.

Recovering enough to begin the session, she again looked out at her audience and thanked them for coming on such short notice. This would be an informal information exchange, she announced, and questions and comments would be welcome at any time. "I also would like to encourage everyone to share observations or stories about what you have felt, seen or heard as it relates to the climate and productivity of your organization," she said.

"After giving some thought to the easiest way to structure this exchange, it boiled down to seven lessons about dealing with this type of significant change in an organization." With that, she placed her outline on the computer screen as Harry had instructed, and the computer transferred the words onto the huge wall screen:

THE LESSONS

1 SURVIVOR SYNDROME: A SICKNESS THAT AFFECTS THE 4 PS: PROFITABILITY, PRODUCTIVITY, PERFORMANCE AND PERSONAL HEALTH

2 INTEGRATING THE NEEDS OF BUSINESS, EMPLOYEES AND COMMUNITY

3 COACHING YOURSELF AND OTHERS

4 WHAT'S DRIVING DOWNSIZING STRATEGY

5 MINIMIZING THE EFFECTS OF NEGATIVE EMOTIONS AND BEHAVIORS

6 BENEFITING FROM THE CHANGING EMPLOYMENT RELATIONSHIP

7 BUILDING PERSONAL INDEPENDENCE AND EMPLOYABILITY

Turning her attention back to the group, she continued, "If there is something I don't touch on that you feel is important, please ask about it. If I don't know the answer, maybe we can all figure it out together." She smiled; watched as some of them appeared to relax. Then they were off.

☆ ☆ ☆ ☆

"Survivor Syndrome is the term used to describe the attitudes, beliefs and behaviors exhibited by employees after a significant downsizing has occurred," Stephanie said. "And let me point out, just so you don't miss it, that as Chief of your company, each of you also is a survivor. It's not just the employees you supervise."

She waited a moment, allowing the group to absorb the thought. "On Earth, we define the act of 'surviving' as the ability to exist in spite of adversity. So it seems natural that employees remaining in the chaos of an organization attempting to redefine itself after a downsizing be viewed as survivors.

"There is a group of common symptoms that result in a pattern of behavior exhibited after a downsizing is initiated. That's why the term 'syndrome' is used, she said. "Until recently, the term 'Survivor Syndrome' has been used only when referring to employees in those organizations that have downsized. However, I'm beginning to see organizations back on Earth in which symptoms are present even though a downsizing hasn't taken place. I believe the reason for this is that employees everywhere have been so exposed to the practice and stories of downsizing through interactions with family members, neighbors, news reports and general conversation, that they are being affected vicariously."

Stephanie surveyed the room, pleased to see that her audience was attentive. Then she continued. "What our employees believe and perceive directly influences their attitude, which in turn drives their behavior and, ultimately, their performance.

"For us on Earth, one of the most important things to realize about Survivor Syndrome is that it is firmly rooted in the concept of the 'psychological contract.' That is, that employees who worked hard, were dedicated, sacrificed whatever it took, were loyal and were committed, would be taken care of by the company until they resigned or retired. That belief, and never mind that it's merely implied, is called a psychological contract.

"This psychological contract was never on paper. It was never signed by employee and employer. Still, it was strongly implied by maternal policies and procedures promoted by the company. So for us on Earth, as we better understand the past employment relationship and the resultant situation brought on by terminating the psychological contract, we can see why, as business leaders, we are responsible for helping ourselves and our employees manage this change. We all must learn about Survivor Syndrome and how to immunize against it.

"If, after you learn about it, you decide not to help your employees, you must realize that they will seek their own understanding and take the necessary steps to cure themselves — with your help or without it."

☆ ☆ ☆ ☆

The Chiefs seemed to consider Stephanie as they listened to her speak. At five-foot two and weighing little more than a feather, she was not the world's most imposing figure. In fact, what she was armed with was an impish grin, a light dusting of freckles on her nose and a short, strawberry blonde page-boy. Some thought she looked like an elf — one that, as soon as she opened her mouth, made it very clear that her knowl-edge gave her all the authority she needed to be taken seri-ously.

"On Earth, this practice of loyalty to a company in return for job security started back in the '50s. I can remember my parents lecturing me about not being a 'job hopper.' That was the kiss of death for any resume. Instead, it was, 'Start with a good company and work hard, and they'll take care of you.' That's what my dad used to tell me."

How many of them had heard something similar? she asked. About three-quarters of the audience raised their hands. "So you see, even though we live in different worlds now, our worlds are a lot more similar than they appear to be, " she replied.

All hands went down except one. Stephanie acknowledged its owner. "I'm confused," the Chief said, rising from his seat. "What can we do about this contract — excuse me, this *virtual* contract? We never signed anything. We never told them they could stay forever. Our employees can see what's happening in our industry. Why can't they adjust their attitudes and move on? Why are they so paralyzed?

"Bottom line is, if they don't like it here, leave," he said. "We'll find someone else to take their place. They're not leaving, though. They just stay and make those around them miserable. Every day, it's a challenge for their supervisor, brought on by their complaints, resistance and their eternal search for someone to blame."

It was a good question, though Stephanie had expected it. "Let's look at the symptoms of Survivor Syndrome as I answer your question," she replied, head bent over the tablet as she prepared another list:

SYMPTOMS OF SURVIVOR SYNDROME

- ☆ INSECURE ABOUT JOB
- ☆ FEAR OF THE UNKNOWN
- ☆ MISTRUST OF MANAGEMENT
- ☆ FEAR OF FINANCIAL LOSS
- ☆ UNCERTAIN OF SKILLS AND ABILITIES
- ☆ LACK OF LOYALTY
- ☆ HIGH STRESS LEVELS
- ☆ LOW SELF-ESTEEM
- ☆ DEPENDENT ON THE COMPANY FOR VALIDATION

When she finished writing, she turned to the list that was now, reflected on the huge floating screen. "These are the primary symptoms many employees feel when the company they have trusted, worked hard for and believed in injects the reality of job instability by announcing layoffs, restructuring, a merger, or some significant change to the culture that fostered them in the past. And remember," Stephanie cautioned, "that can be *anyone* from the top position to the bottom position, and everyone in between. It doesn't matter how good the reasons are for making the decision to downsize. All the worker knows is that the organization of the past, the one they knew and trusted, has just changed the rules, big-time. Suddenly they're unsure of their future."

Stephanie hesitated. "Now, let's be honest," she said. "Isn't 'downsizing' really just another word for 'firing?' Aren't we really *firing* employees for reasons other than poor performance? Employees who have been part of the corporate family? We're really not 'letting them go' with the expectation of bringing them back at some point, are we? So why call it something that it's not?

"Remember what I said earlier," she said as she glanced around the large room. "Chiefs, officers and managers have feelings, too. And sometimes, because they're struggling with changes they're responsible for carrying out, it's easier to do what is unpleasant if it's sugar-coated. That's where words like 'layoffs' come from. Or 'downsizing,' or 'rightsizing.' It's too difficult for us to say that we're 'firing 1/3 of our work force.' We know in our hearts these employees have done nothing wrong. Calling it 'firing' would be too harsh for us to live with, as well as too harsh for them to hear.

"To make matters worse," Stephanie continued, "often, because our managers aren't ready or trained to deal with these significant changes on a personal or professional level, downsizing takes place in a manner that excludes respect and dignity. To add more fuel to the fire, at least on Earth, many

CEOs draw huge bonuses while workers in the trenches are being slashed. Not a pleasant picture, whatever angle you view it from."

Stephanie stared into the numb expressions before her. "Are you starting to see what the internal survivor, the employee who stays with the organization after downsizing, is dealing with?" she asked, with empathy in her voice. "So often, executives believe they need to focus on taking care of the employees they are letting go, even as they think employees who are staying should be grateful they still have a job. It's like this gentleman stated: If they don't like it, they can leave.

"Trouble is, they're not ready to leave. And in many cases, they're not capable of it."

☆ ☆ ☆ ☆

Stephanie stepped out from behind the podium and moved down to the floor to walk among the Chiefs. "Research shows that both internal survivors — those who stay on after layoffs — and external survivors — those who are being let go — share the same emotions and feelings about the changes they are experiencing. Think about that, and tell me: How many of you offer some type of help to employees being let go? Either severance, job-search skills or counseling?"

Almost every hand in the room went up.

"How many of you offer similar help to internal survivors? Training for new skills needed in the new organization? Instructions on dealing with change on a professional level as well as a personal one? Information about emotional response and how to handle change? Who among you have provided them with a glimpse of how *they* can build a bridge for themselves to ease the transition from the previous organizational culture to the new one?"

No hands went up.

"Don't be embarrassed if your firm has not proactively addressed internal survivor issues," she replied. "If someone had asked me that question four years ago, I would have responded the same way. In fact, four years ago, my company also had very senior executives saying the very same words I've heard you say: 'If they don't like it, they can leave.'

"But what we saw time and time again were employees who didn't like what was happening, but who weren't prepared to leave, either. So they stayed and continued to resist change because they were fearful of the future. This resistance cost us a lot of money and a lot of lost time.

"What we learned, and I suggest you consider, is that employees are not totally to blame for the attitudes and beliefs they hold. Each employee, with the help and encouragement of management — at least on Earth and since the end of World War II — has contributed to an attitude of entitlement.

"Consider the evolution of the employment relationship on Earth." As she related a brief chronological history of management theories that helped to shape the current relationship, Stephanie passed among the tables of Chiefs. "Prior to the Industrial Revolution, management motivated by some form of fear or punishment. Then, with the arrival of the Industrial Revolution and the influence of a less personal relationship, the theories of Frederick Taylor, the 'father of management theory' were embraced. Taylor believed that trained workers were motivated by their need for money. He made assumptions about workers that led management to believe they needed closer supervision and routine.

By the late 1920s, Taylor's ideas and the practice of "piecemeal" rates dissolved as the work force reacted to an era of mass production. Naturally, management thinking also changed. Researchers argued the importance of considering the 'whole person' on the job. The existence and strength of informal work groups were identified and greater attention was paid to employing group-incentive systems. Management thinking gave way to the human relations model, based on the social process. The relationship had developed to one in which the supervisor was more understanding and sympathetic to the needs of the subordinates. But because management was still using strategies aimed at securing employee compliance through managerial authority, it was short-lived.

"The human resources model was the next to evolve, declaring that workers were motivated by a complex set of interrelated factors. This model was unique in that it recognized that different employees seek different goals in any one job, and that they offer a diversity of talents to the workplace. As a result, management no longer manipulated employees to accept authority. Instead, they created an environment that allowed employees to successfully meet their own goals and, at the same time, meet those of the organization. This basically is where we are today."

Stepping back on stage, Stephanie looked at her audience. "The important thing to remember is that, as history demonstrates, the employee-employer relationship continues to evolve and mature to fit and serve the nature of the way work is being performed.

✩ ✩ ✩ ✩

As she spoke, images began to appear on the overhead screen, photos Stephanie had selected from a cyberspace archive when she prepared her meeting notes. The first to emerge was an enormous image of Rosie the Riveter — rolled-up sleeve revealing a muscled arm and providing an amusing contrast to the petite Stephanie.

"During World War II, we called on all Americans to come forward and do their duty for government and country. After the war was over," she said, projecting a slide of a 1950s-era subdivision, complete with car in every driveway, "it was common for Americans to expect a good job and good salaries, with annual increases every year. These pay increases were expected just for showing up. There was no measurement of performance or contribution, because" — here, a trio of slides depicting busy American factories, shipyards, and farmlands — "America had a huge dominance in the marketplace.

"America was confident her leadership in the military and supply market would never be challenged. That attitude trickled down to American management, and down to the workers from there. That's where workers got their sense of entitlement. Many still continue to cling to it today."

Stephanie walked over to the table and poured herself a glass of water. "Because things were going well, and American companies felt they would always be the leaders in their industries, companies often looked the other way when employees weren't contributing or pulling their own weight. Naturally, employees surmised that they could do minimal work and hold on to both their job and the American dream. Because the organization was so maternal, it was accepted that management must take care of all employees, regardless of whether they were making a contribution. They were family.

"But today, the rules of the game have changed," she said, returning to the podium.

Stephanie rubbed the short hair at the nape of her neck and considered the big screen, on which she had again displayed the symptoms of Survivor Syndrome. "Let's look at how the symptoms of Survivor Syndrome manifest themselves in the behaviors you observe in your employees, and possibly in yourself. Remember, you're a survivor, too."

BEHAVIORS

☆ NARROW-MINDED

☆ AVERSION TO RISK-TAKING

☆ LOW PRODUCTIVITY

☆ DEPRESSED

☆ INCREASED ABSENTEEISM

☆ LOW MORALE

☆ LOSS OF PRIDE IN COMPANY

☆ INCREASED RESISTANCE TO CHANGE

☆ ACTS OF SABOTAGE

"These are behaviors typically seen in survivors," she said. "Look at them. Can you see why they are paralyzing to you and your co-workers? No wonder Survivor Syndrome negatively affects the company's performance, the resultant profitability analysis, productivity, and the personal health and wellness of employees.

"Let me ask you a question," she said, directing the request at a Chief sitting at the back of the room. "Have you had to lay off any of your employees yet?"

The gentleman stood up and introduced himself as Pete Grover, Chief of 25th-Century Security Software. His company used to be at the forefront of leading-edge technology for cyberspace security, he told her. Many of his clients were financial and lending institutions. And "yes," he said, his shoulders drooping as if in imitation of Harry's earlier stance. "Yes, we decided to downsize about two years ago when the banking industry was going through such substantial change and our client base was reduced by half. Somehow, we didn't see it coming — at least not the way the changes were going to affect us.

"A lot of the things you mentioned really describe my company. We never thought about new market segments until it was much too late."

His voice was filled with frustration. "Now we can't get our employees to be creative and take risks with their ideas like they used to," he lamented. "It's so difficult for them to trust their managers, and their managers are getting frustrated, too, ramming their heads against the wall and getting nowhere. It's getting so bad, I'm beginning to hear my best managers make statements like, 'If they don't like it, let them leave.' But that's not the kind of culture I want at 25th-Century. I'm just not sure what I can do to help them all, I've been feeling so frustrated.

"But I certainly do have a better idea about why I'm seeing this behavior. I'm glad I decided to take Harry up on this session."

Stephanie recognized the pain on Pete's face as he spoke. She had seen it in her own company. "As Harry mentioned in my introduction, I have been intimately involved in this topic of downsizing, or firing, or layoffs, or whatever we want to call it," she said. "I can relate to the pain I see on Pete's face and on the faces of so many of you. I also have struggled with the feelings of helplessness — knowing on one hand it's my job to aid my company through this transition and, on the other, realizing I can't drag workers to their stations every day and make them be productive."

Looking directly at Pete, she said, "As we explore this topic together, I hope you'll learn how to recreate a work relationship that is built on mutual respect, independence and good work."

Stephanie again moved out from behind the podium and stepped down to the floor. "Ten years ago, as a member of the management team, I was focused on all the prosperity we were enjoying. So much so, that my arrogance acted as a sort of blindfold and I didn't see the future that was coming. That's why my journey over the past six years has been such a steep learning curve. I began with intense study of this topic, along with interviews with former and current employees. From those discussions, I adopted a model for strategic planning when downsizing is a possibility. I've learned to support training and assistance for internal survivors to complement what we do for external survivors. I came to realize that we needed to balance the training for those staying with the level of preparedness we were providing for those leaving. It only makes sense to do this, because the internal survivors are the ones we're counting on to take the company into a profitable future.

42

"I've found all these things are important to focus on, because Survivor Syndrome acts like a thief. It can rob your company of productivity, committed and dependable employees, quality of product, and morale. It creates greater absenteeism and higher costs associated with any employee assistance program offered. In addition, the poor spirit that the work place exudes negatively affects the ability to recruit new employees. All this adds up to inefficient management spending."

As she spoke, Pete watched and listened intently. He was impressed with Stephanie's willingness to speak to the Chiefs, despite her harrowing trip to Virtual Cove. He knew from experience that cyberspace travel can be exhausting. The passion she felt for this topic was obvious, as was her desire to find humane ways to take the bitter edge off the reality of downsizing. He was glad he had decided to accept Harry's invitation. He only hoped he would have the opportunity to get to know Stephanie better. Perhaps she would even be willing to help him conquer the insidious syndrome that had been eroding morale at his own company.

☆ ☆ ☆ ☆

43

LESSON TWO

Integrating the Needs of Business, Employees and Community

Lesson One   Survivor Syndrome: A Sickness that
Affects the 4 Ps

Lesson Two   Integrating the Needs of Business,
Employees and Community

Stephanie moved back to the cartoon-rocket podium and peered out at her audience. "Because many of you have indicated you are practicing a less-than-formal process for developing and implementing a downsizing strategy, I'd like to share with you a model that will help you develop win-win strategies for your firms." As if on cue, the model (Figure 1) appeared on the wall screen:

Integrated Downsizing Approach - IDA

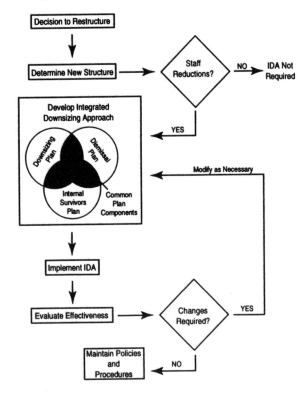

"This is called the Integrated Downsizing Approach, or IDA," she said, using the laser pointer to indicate different elements. "The purpose of this model is to clarify the various plans and elements of preparation that should be considered, in concert with one another, if the development of a downsizing strategy is called for.

"I'd like for you to think of this model as a three-legged stool. Without all three legs, the stool is no good — it'll just wobble and fall over. Without these three elements present in your approach to a strategy, your organization is destined for the same fate. It will wobble. And it will fail to meet the established goals for the new organization."

Stephanie selected the next slide (Figure 2) to appear on the wall.

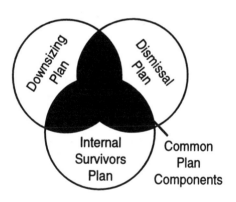

Then she left the platform and walked to the center of the room. Using the laser pointer, she highlighted "Downsizing Plan."

"Let's start at the very beginning. Just because your company decides to restructure, it doesn't necessarily mean a downsizing will take place. However, as part of that restructuring process, systems should be reviewed. Usually, as a result of the review, some change is called for, and sometimes, it's a reduction of the number of employees performing tasks. What the downsizing plan is designed to do is give you and your employees the opportunity to explore options.

"Now I understand that not every company is going to have the luxury of a years' notice, or even six months. Sometimes, action must be taken immediately after the decision to change performance or direction is made," she said.

Indicating the circle depicting the downsizing plan, she continued, "This is the time when you design the plan that fits your expectations and time line. This is a time to research alternative measures, and examine options such as early retirement and attrition. In fact," she added, strolling the aisles, "some companies have had extraordinary success with gathering their employees together, putting the cards directly on the table and asking them for their thoughts and help with determining which actions the company should take.

"You'd be surprised by the answers they get," Stephanie said, a smile in her voice. "Often, employees are willing to volunteer for other assignments, take a leave of absence to go back to school, or request part-time status so they can pursue other interests that they've been putting off in order to save the company from having to actually cut jobs.

"The purpose of this plan also is to define the scope of the downsizing — clarify why a particular plan has been chosen and determine specifics about how the downsizing plan will be communicated. And when I say *communicated*, I mean the 'whys,' 'hows,' 'whens' and 'by whoms.'"

Stephanie stopped, finding herself standing next to Les Cook. Les was the chief from Cybertain, a large media and

46

entertainment company. "Let me ask you all a question," she stated. "How would you grade your organization? Did you do a good job with your own downsizing plan? If not, what would you do differently?

"And are you open to asking your employees for feedback about how to improve the process you've selected if, in fact, you have to again downsize in the future?" A pause. Stephanie looked around the room, aware of the discomfort her questions had created.

It was Les who broke the silence. "Stephanie, I'm not sure you want to know the answer — I mean, about how we would grade ourselves. I know I'd do it differently if I had to do it again. But how? Can you give us some clearer direction of how to make this happen?"

"Sure, Les," she replied, making her way back to the podium. Using the laserwriter, she wrote the following words on the computer tablet; again, they appeared on the wall:

- ☆ JOB ANALYSIS
- ☆ JOB TRAINING AND RETRAINING
- ☆ EMPLOYEE RELATIONS
- ☆ RESEARCH
- ☆ FINANCIAL IMPACT

"Let's take these one by one." Pointing to the first item, she continued, "It's important to do some type of job analysis of functions and tasks that will continue after the restructuring and re-engineering are complete. Ask yourselves: What specific skills will the organization require? What skills are no longer needed? How do these needs match the current pool of employees the organization has to draw from? Naturally, you will want to do as much planning up front as possible, to match remaining jobs to employees possessing the skills and experience to do them. But don't overlook job retraining and job rotation as other viable methods to ultimately match employees and jobs."

Stephanie moved the pointer to the second item. "Now training — that's an interesting topic," she said, a grin lighting up her petite face. "Not only do you have to determine what kind of training your employees will need to manage the company successfully in the future, you also need to figure out which employees are even interested and have the best attitude to take on training. And, of course, where you are cross-training employees or planning job retraining, you need to give some thought to marketing the approaches so employees will recognize the long-term benefit of continuous learning.

"I've listed employee relations," she said, highlighting the next point on the wall, "because I strongly believe it is important for the team developing the downsizing plan to be cognitive of the current climate, the history of change for the company and/or business unit, as well as the current relationship that exists between employees and senior management. Being aware of these elements will assist the organization with determining successful strategies for communicating the plan.

Stephanie returned to the stage. "The last two elements should not be underrated," she said, leaning forward to grip the edge of the podium as she spoke. She was becoming so relaxed with the Chiefs, she had almost forgotten that she was somewhere in cyberspace, floating among stars and planets. "I know that when companies are considering downsizing, they often frown on calling on compatriots from other companies to talk about lessons learned. But there are ways to research and learn from the mistakes of others. Remember: People are people. For the most part, they want to be treated as adults, with dignity, respect and compassion. So even if the industry or set of circumstances are slightly different, focus on lessons that address human reaction. Then walk away with a plan that promotes good organizational citizenship and a realistic financial plan. The financial plan should estimate the savings in the short and long run, even as it earmarks adequate funds to support the transition of external survivors to new work — and take the internal survivors to the new vision.

"As we wrap up the downsizing plan, let's focus on the outcomes of a successful plan. What benefits could your company derive from implementing a thorough plan at this level?" Stephanie asked, eyes sweeping the room in search of a volunteer.

Harry was the first to speak. "Well, Stephanie, I would hope we would have a clear purpose to relay to our employees. But I think it's more important that management puts itself through such a thorough soul-searching in the process of developing that purpose, they'll be preparing themselves to deal with all the reactions. I've seen my management, including myself, become less visible and less accessible after the decision was announced. I think that's because we just don't feel we can adequately express why that approach was selected."

"Thanks, Harry."

Someone from the other side of the room spoke up. "I'd be pleased knowing we had done everything possible to prepare our managers to take on the responsibility of letting staff go, and I think the actions also would result in the managers feeling better and, ultimately, our employees being treated more fairly." It was Sally Creekman speaking. Harry had pointed her out earlier in the morning: She was Chief of the Jetting Arena. Her responsibilities included managing what on Earth are known as hotels and restaurants, for metropolitan Virtual Cove and the surrounding cyberspace.

"The comments I've fielded from my employees are twofold," Sally said. "The managers who had to carry out the order to downsize reported that they were not prepared — not prepared for the emotional trauma they would see, and not prepared for what they would feel. They also didn't feel we had adequate procedures to consistently inform our employees of company policies and benefits. I'm glad you had training on your list, Stephanie, because I know from the experience we've already had that training our managers needs to be right up there on the list of priorities for the future, as well as training for the employees who remain.

"On the other hand," she mused, "I've had lots of comments from employees who remained with the firm, or 'internal survivors,' as you put it. They're worried about our organization's citizenship role. When we downsized, it was — like so many of the firms represented here today — our first time. We were somewhat embarrassed that it had come to this. We wanted to do it, hide our heads in the sand and forget it happened. With that kind of management attitude, you can imagine how poorly we stood up to our citizenship role.

"We definitely would do things differently in the future. I'm glad to see that your comments support our findings," she concluded, and sat down.

Stephanie thanked her. "There are two more things I'd like you to consider as outcomes of downsizing," she addressed the group. "First, this is a time to consider security issues. And then there's the impact your company's announcement is going to have on the communities it supports. Don't forget that the loss of jobs from your business will affect many other businesses in your community, from fast food diners to the clothing shops to the home builders.

"Well, enough about the downsizing plan. Let's move on to the dismissal plan."

Stephanie changed the slide and the three rings reappeared on the screen. Pointing to the trio, she said, "The key to IDA is realizing that all three of these plans are being developed in concert with one another." She looked out into the sea of Chiefs to make sure they understood her point. "What I mean by that is, although different employees may be participating on each of the three development teams, they must all be aware of the plans that are being developed simultaneously and consider those plans as they structure their specific action steps.

"The method by which this information is shared can take many forms. Perhaps they meet weekly to provide each other with updates, or use computer technology to confidentially share necessary information. Whatever is decided, contact should be sufficient if it is to result in a seamless trio of plans that do not take on the characteristics of having been developed in the dark, independent of one another.

"Let's look at dismissal," Stephanie repeated. "The purpose of this plan is to decide on severance and what financial impact it will have on the organization. This also is the time to discuss and determine if outplacement support and services will be provided to those being asked to leave. Generally you will find that most employees have not begun a job search, especially at the initial stages of the downsizing effort. These employees will be overwhelmed, and could be experiencing shock from the announcement, so it's almost unreasonable to expect that they will have the capacity to immediately focus on securing new employment. Therefore, any help you can offer to deal with their emotional state first represents time well-spent. Not only does this expedite the re-employment process, it establishes goodwill with internal survivors and the community as they examine the treatment the staff is receiving."

Stephanie was beginning to feel fatigued, so she perched herself on a tall stool that looked like a fixture from a 23rd-century barroom. When she had comfortably situated herself on the multicolored seat, she continued. "I'm not sure what the legal climate is here in Virtual Cove, but back on Earth there are several other important components of the dismissal plan. First and foremost is the clear definition of how dismissals will be determined," she said. "This varies by company, depending on the types of skills needed, the length of employment of the staff, the technical nature of the work, and so on. Some organizations have successfully developed a formula considering longevity, skills and performance.

"Whatever you decide, it should be clearly documented, easy to follow and consistently practiced."

Stephanie turned her attention to the Jetting Arena Chief. "Just as Sally shared, it is important for your managers to know what the process will be for dismissing an employee. That process should be documented, and it should be sensitive to the dignity of both employer and employee. Remember, the world is watching. Would you like to see this process played out on the evening news?

"One last point about the dismissal plan: This also is a time to consider what action to take if a situation arises that threatens the security of the manager, other employees or the firm."

Pete, the software Chief, eyed Stephanie. There she was, a tiny but wise princess atop a tall throne before her captivated subjects. It was silly, he knew. Strictly fairy-tale stuff. But I can't help it, he thought. That's *exactly* what she reminds me of.

Pete was struck by her compassion for humanity, and her ability to articulate her thoughts and relate her experience. Also inviting admiration was that she had immediately established an atmosphere in which the Chiefs, perfect strangers all, were comfortable sharing their thoughts and feelings.

He was pulled into his reverie only temporarily, accompanied by Stephanie's sweet, clear voice acknowledging questions and soliciting feedback. Then, forcing his attention back to the present, he was inexplicably inspired to stand and speak. He had vaguely heard Stephanie's question about the benefits to be derived from the dismissal plan, but personal experience would provide an acceptable answer. Besides, though he'd never admit it, even to himself, he wanted her to notice him.

He cleared his throat and began. "Based on my experience," he stated, "the thing that impressed me about the dismissal plan is the importance of offering a well-defined strategy of selecting employees for dismissal. We really had some problems at this point when we initiated our plan. Now I understand why. It should clearly not be hinged on 'who's friends with the boss.' It needs to realistically and thoroughly review potential liabilities of the dismissal action.

"You referred to the legal climate on Earth" — this, as he looked directly at Stephanie. "From what I can remember about that climate, I would say that Virtual Cove has not approached Earth's litigious pace. Of course, that's not to say that things like downsizing won't change that."

As Pete took his seat, Josh Evans, who had been leaning against the far wall, straightened up and introduced himself as the Chief of the largest clothing manufacturer within light years of Virtual Cove. "Seems to me," he said, walking closer, "that these issues of severance and outplacement must also be documented and communicated to all employees — those leaving as well as those staying. I know I'd sure like to see some financial support if I was attempting to re-establish myself. I think the benefit we would see would come from clearly communicating our plan, to avoid gaps that the grapevine then fills in.

"But what is offered and what formula is applied must be seriously studied in light of the firm's financial capabilities," he pointed out. "We offered outplacement support to some of our senior folks, but I clearly see the mistake we made by failing to provide everyone with basic help on things like preparing resumes, interviewing and networking. I know we'd do that differently the next time." With that, he returned to the wall and resumed his position.

As Stephanie listened to the group voice their opinions and observations, it occurred to her that she had unfinished business in Atlanta. There, internal survivors with whom she had been working were also worried about their future. She made a mental note to ask them for some feedback on the programs she had introduced, to determine if those programs were addressing their needs and easing fears of what the unknown future had to offer. Stephanie was committed to helping them realize their full potential and the actual transferability of their skills. She also noted that she wanted to explore the process other organizations went through in establishing in-house career development centers. Perhaps that was a possibility for her firm.

Either way, she decided, it was just one more step in providing the resources for her employees to build their bridge to tomorrow.

"This last leg of the stool is the plan for addressing the needs of internal survivors," she continued, using the laser pointer to direct the group's attention to the internal survivor circle. "The purpose of this plan is to define the new employment contract in terms that align with the company's new vision and mission. Your team will want to structure the revision of policies and procedures to mirror the roles and expectations of the new organization. This will be the place to explore performance expectations and how employees will be held accountable for their contributions. The team assigned to address internal survivor issues will need to consider how the reward and recognition plans will change to encourage the behavior you are looking for, as well as help survivors deal with their emotions and the impact on themselves and their families."

As Stephanie said these words, she was remembering a day back on Earth when she had been working with a group of survivors in her communications firm. She had been facilitating a small group session when one of the employees had remarked, "It's like my best friend died, but I couldn't talk to anyone about it." The pain she heard in that woman's voice and saw on her face was unmistakable. She also remembered how helpless she felt. She knew the only answer was to help this woman, and other survivors like her, understand what was happening to her. Only through self-discovery would she be able to accept the current situation and take control of her own destiny, but Stephanie knew she would need help with that, too. By concentrating on learning a few new skills and opening themselves up to a different way of thinking, they could move into the future as more independent workers, aware of their value.

55

Turning her attention back to the Chiefs, she continued. "Some of the tasks included at this stage call for investigating downsizing practices set by other companies, practices that are humane and fair; identifying training and counseling to help internal survivors accept the situation; educating your workers so they can construct action plans for moving forward; and creating a culture and work environment that encourages and rewards employees who enable themselves to be risk-takers and creative thinkers. This is the place to design interventions that will help employees see their worth and lay out a road map to get themselves to the future.

"As we've done with the other two plans, let me ask you again: What are the key benefits from this plan?" Stephanie asked, glancing around the room.

This time, Linda was the first speak.

"Just as we said with the external survivors, I believe one of the most important things we all would benefit from is being clear and forthright with the internal survivors in communicating the new culture and mission of the firm," she replied. "The sooner this is understood and incorporated into everyday work practices, the sooner the business can again gain momentum. I think it also is important for them to know what their role is. However, I believe this will be a continuous project, not just 'once, and done.' Stephanie, I wonder if you have any comments about that?"

Stephanie chewed her lip, contemplating the question. "You're right, Linda," she finally replied. "Working with internal survivors will be a continuous process, for the firm as well as for the survivor who is exploring how to redefine himself or herself. The survivor will be exploring what her passions are and what excites her about work. She also will be capturing the true essence of what she values in life. So often, in the old patriarchal organization, the worker's values and beliefs were suppressed for so long that they lost touch with them. It takes time to rediscover these feelings. That's why this team, and each and every survivor, must be prepared for courageous work — work that will evolve over time. The pace will be different for each individual, depending on how comfortable they are with dealing with the results of their self-discovery work."

Harry had been sitting back in his chair, absorbing this information. In fact, he looked so relaxed that Stephanie was beginning to wonder if he was really listening or if he had somehow tuned into some cosmic meditation music. As if he had read her mind, he jumped up and seized the moment to offer his observations — but not without almost upsetting his chair. Stephanie had to laugh to herself. The scene reminded her of his earlier conspicuous awkwardness.

Harry recovered and began, unfazed. "Sitting here listening has helped me realize one big piece that we either have overlooked or purposely sidestepped at Virtual Travel," he ventured. "We need to open up communications and look for ways to better share information, both upward and downward. We need to begin rebuilding trust by being accessible. And if there's anything we need, it's to stop choosing our words so carefully that the message is shrouded. Right now our employees need a map to understand what's being said. This whole idea of communications needs work. I'd like to see the day that when the employee, if she doesn't have the information needed, feels empowered to ask for it without the fear of being reprimanded."

Harry sat back in his chair, and a very tall woman with a head full of long dark curls stood. One of the things her company was struggling with was helping employees understand the basics of change management, she said. As she related her concerns, she began to pace the floor, as if in unconscious imitation of Stephanie.

"We really need to help our internal survivors deal with all these changes in their lives. I know plenty of workers who not only are juggling changes at work, but are trying to find time and energy to deal with changes at home, like with kids and aging parents. Some of these people still have family on Earth, and it's a chore getting enough time off to return for a visit. I think we can be most helpful assisting these survivors to better understand and manage their capacity for change, through better education of what change is."

Stephanie smiled an acknowledgment. "I thank you all for your attention and interpretation of how these pieces would fit in your organizations. Now let's turn our attention to the common area of this three-legged stool." With that, another slide flashed onto the wall:

Common
Components

"I'd like to list the many elements that are common to all three plans and recommend that you consider them all, in terms of each plan I've listed." One by one, they appeared on the wall as she announced them:

- ☆ PERCEPTION OF ORGANIZATIONAL CITIZENSHIP ROLE

- ☆ OPPORTUNITY TO GRIEVE

- ☆ NURTURING EMPLOYEES TO BE ENABLED FOR THE FUTURE

- ☆ ENCOURAGING CONTINUOUS LEARNING

- ☆ DEMONSTRATING A COMMITMENT TO THE NEW EMPLOYMENT RELATIONSHIP

- ☆ RECOGNIZING THAT INDIVIDUALS HAVE DIFFER-ENT CAPACITIES FOR CHANGE

- ☆ DON'T GO TOO FAST WITH INITIATING THE CHANGE

- ☆ DON'T GO TOO SLOW WITH IT, EITHER

- ☆ ESTABLISHING REALISTIC COST ESTIMATES AND TIME FRAMES FOR ACTION

- ☆ GENERATE BUY-IN AND COMMITMENT

- ☆ COMMUNICATE FREQUENTLY

- ☆ UPDATE PROCEDURES AS NECESSARY

When she finished, Stephanie turned to her audience. "Remember, all of these activities should be integrated into each and every plan of this approach. No part should be devoid of these values."

LESSON THREE

Coaching Yourself and Others

"...I say all that to ask, What can we do to help ourselves be ready to deal with these issues?"

With a start, Pete awoke. He had allowed himself to drift into a daydream, and returned to the present in time to catch Paul Smith, Chief of Condos of the Future, mid-sentence. Apparently, more than a few moments had passed since his imagination had taken over and given his mind license to wander. Where the hell are we with this? he wondered. Just as he had decided it was futile to guess, at least accurately, what was being discussed, Stephanie came to the rescue.

60

"Now let me see if I understand your question," she said, thoughtfully. "You're experiencing some of the Survivor Syndrome symptoms I've described and you also are realizing that before you can help others, you have to be able to deal with this yourself. The question is, how? Is that what you're asking?" Her eye caught Pete's and they both smiled, co-conspirators.

"Yeah, that's right," replied Paul. "Shouldn't I help myself first?"

"You bet you should! I'm so impressed," Stephanie enthused. "I really am. Because that's exactly what has to happen. It is extremely difficult, if not impossible, for you or any of your managers to exhibit and demonstrate the best attitudes and behaviors if you don't first deal with some of your own personal feelings about the changes."

Stephanie picked up a few computer-style tablets and a fistful of the funny pens with the tips that glowed. Making her way up and down the aisles, she distributed one to each table as the Chiefs watched with some curiosity. "We're going to do a little exercise, for which you will work in small groups at your tables," she explained. "Everyone has an assignment, though I want only one individual to speak at a time. While that person is speaking, everyone else has the job of being quiet and listening. When the speaker is finished, the person on his or her right will pause for a moment and then make their brief statement, and so on.

"Listening, if you're doing it right, is a lot of work," she continued. "I don't want you to think about how you would respond to the person speaking. And I don't want you to be thinking about what you're going to say when your turn comes. Instead, I want you to hear with your eyes, your ears and your heart the message being shared by your colleague.

"Now, I don't want you to talk about just anything. I have a specific topic. Your assignment is to share one observation or feeling about how downsizing has affected you.

"I'll give you 20 minutes for this exercise. When everyone at your table has had a chance to speak, I'd like one volunteer at each table to scribe a list of the common themes expressed through the exercise." Stephanie surveyed the room. "Does anyone have any questions about what I'm asking you to do? Okay, then. Go ahead and get started."

Stephanie was impressed with the group's enthusiasm. Experience suggested this intervention was an opportunity for participants to free themselves of frustration and pain. As she had predicted, the Chiefs delved into the assignment, relieved to be taking part in a sort of mass catharsis.

Watching as the groups' designated secretaries scribbled lists and the words appeared on the walls, Stephanie was reminded again that it doesn't matter which galaxy one calls home, feelings can be universal:

☆ IT WAS TOO PAINFUL TO FIRE PEOPLE WHO WERE DOING A GOOD JOB JUST BECAUSE THE BUSINESS HAD NOT BEEN PAYING ATTENTION TO THE WARNING SIGNS

☆ I FELT LIKE I WAS BETRAYING MY BEST FRIEND

☆ IT IS DIFFICULT FOR ME TO COME TO TERMS WITH WHY I'M STILL EMPLOYED AND MY CO-WORKERS, WHO NEEDED THE JOB MORE THAN I DID, ARE GONE

☆ I FELT BAD BECAUSE WE DIDN'T DO ANYTHING TO HELP OUR EMPLOYEES PREPARE FOR THIS NEW WORK RELATIONSHIP. IT WAS LIKE WE JUST ABANDONED THEM

☆ I'M NOT SURE WHAT I SHOULD BE DOING ABOUT MY FUTURE. I'M SCARED OF THE UNKNOWN

☆ WE USED TO BE FAMILY. THIS ISN'T THE WAY FAMILY SHOULD TREAT FAMILY

☆ AFTER DEALING WITH EMOTIONS CONNECTED TO FIRING AND INSECURITY ABOUT THE FUTURE, I FEEL DRAINED OF THE ENERGY REQUIRED TO DO MY JOB

☆ HOW DO I GET MY FEELINGS UNDER CONTROL? ONE MINUTE I'M FOCUSING ON OUR NEW ORDERS AND CUSTOMER NEEDS; THE NEXT, I FIND MYSELF SO ANGRY WITH WHAT HAS OCCURRED I COULD SLAM MY FIST THROUGH THE WALL

☆ ☆ ☆ ☆

"So," Stephanie ventured. "What did you think of this exercise?"

Several hands went up. "Well, for one thing I don't feel so alone," offered one woman. "I guess I never had the opportunity to say out loud to others what I was feeling."

"It was like a cleansing," another Chief added. "Never mind that we obviously have feelings — our culture has never focused on them. So we have a tendency to repress our feelings at work. This was good for me, because I realized that a lot of what I've been carrying around has been zapping my energy and affecting my productivity."

The woman with the dark ringlets, who had appeared to retreat into withdrawal during this last exercise, suddenly raised her hand.

"Yes? What were your observations?"

"My name is Rita Pond," the dark-haired woman began. "I'm the Financial Chief for the First Cyberspace Bank. I came to this meeting today to learn more about downsizing for two reasons. First, I personally have feelings about what is happening at First Cyberspace Bank. Second, I played a significant role in making it happen, and I have feelings about that as well.

"Anyway, this exercise helped me realize I can't shoulder the burden for the thousands we had to lay off. There were others in leadership positions. There was our Most High Board, which also was responsible for drafting future business strategies. There were the employees who had a job to do and possibly, because I now am aware of Survivor Syndrome, they might have been unable to change. Nevertheless, they resisted our efforts to change the organization, which slowed the process down and resulted in even more layoffs.

"I see now that I have to concentrate on trying to regain my sense of energy and purpose after having been totally burnt out by this emotionally draining experience. I'd just like to thank Stephanie for asking us to spend some time on this important question," she stammered. "I'm just like some of you. I hadn't stopped to think about everything that was happening and I certainly didn't take time to acknowledge my own feelings. I was so stuck in my guilt that I forgot to pay attention to what was happening to me and to those around me."

Listening to Rita, Stephanie was reminded of the first group of managers at her firm who were asked to discuss a similar topic. Even though that meeting had occurred years ago, the relief expressed then was very similar to what Rita was saying now. Thanking Rita for sharing her observations, she then suggested that everyone reread the lists displayed on the giant wall screens.

After a few moments of silence, she spoke. "Your co-workers and employees are saddled with some of these same feelings," she reminded them. "And as long as these feelings and emotions require energy from them, it will be difficult for them to focus on any new vision you may be suggesting for the future of your company. As long as they're worried about their futures, and stuck not knowing how to take control for themselves, they will not be as efficient and productive as you need them to be.

"Unfortunately, until you and your employees learn to combat Survivor Syndrome, all of you will be paralyzed by some level of fear, guilt, pain and anger. This paralyzing behavior will hold you hostage and adversely affect your ability to meet the firm's goals for productivity, creativity and profitability."

As Stephanie spoke, several members of the audience took notes with the glowing pens. The information she shared seemed rooted in common sense, but as with so many managers on Earth, they had neither taken the time nor found the courage to reflect on it.

Stephanie resumed strolling among the group. "Before we take a break, let's summarize what we have talked about so far." Picking up the laser interpreter, she began to speak into the small recorder, and watched as her words appeared on the screen:

1. REALIZE THE POWER OF YOUR CORPORATE CITIZENSHIP ROLE

"Remember that for every action, decision, memo and meeting, each employee is watching, listening and perhaps reading between the lines in an effort to interpret what you are communicating. Ask yourselves: Do the actions match the words? Do the policies encourage the new behaviors you are looking for? Are employees being treated fairly?

65

"These employees are not the only ones perceiving how your company is preparing for work in the future. So are your customers, the community and your stockholders. We've all seen too much slaughtering, abusive treatment and demoralizing actions, and you can be sure employees, the community and customers are getting sick of it. Don't underestimate the power of customer and stockholder reactions. Commit yourselves to treating people with dignity and respect as a part of your corporate guiding principles. You'll never regret it.

"I'm not sure what statistics you have collected here in Virtual Cove, but back on Earth we lose about 156 million work days a year to depression. That's quite a chunk of change. And the number is rising. Why? In part, it's a direct result of how employees feel about the way they are treated at work."

Stephanie brought the laser interpreter to her lips and read aloud the next item:

2. UNDERSTAND HOW DOWNSIZING AFFECTS THE BUSINESS, EMPLOYEES AND COMMUNITY

"Remember what I said earlier," she reminded. "The emotions employees go through when they are coping with such tremendous changes as downsizing, culture shock and reassignment of work are very similar to those of losing a loved one. In fact" — here she resumed her perpetual pacing — "the psychological community on Earth has done studies that indicate the greatest stress for an individual comes from the death of a loved one; the second-most stressful event is losing a job. What this tells us is not to sell these emotions short. They are there, they are real, and they need to be understood and dealt with.

"Learn how fears about the future are producing these emotions, and remember: Everyone's fears will not be the same, so reactions and behaviors will vary. That's why the interventions, the programs you will design to help change the negative and unproductive behaviors, also will need to vary.

"Employees must learn to trust themselves, as well as truthfully understand their skill level and where those skills and experience can be applied. They must journey to the future knowing solidly what their strengths are and with a plan to strengthen their weaknesses, and commit to continuous learning. They must also be aware and prepared to deal with fears and emotions within their families as the possibility of job loss is discussed."

Stephanie stopped and stood in the middle of the room. "I'm not saying that any of this is easy," she said. "And I'm not saying that turning the situation around will be a quick process. But whether employees believe what the company is doing is right is not important. What's important is to move everyone to acceptance of the situation as quickly as possible. The employee must accept that right or wrong doesn't matter — what matters is that this is the path the company is traveling. Resistance to that journey is unhealthy for them as individuals and detrimental to the survival of the company. Continued resistance to the future will only harm both."

3. PROVIDE OPPORTUNITIES FOR EMPLOYEES TO DISCUSS THEIR EMOTIONS

"Is it possible to gather employees in small groups and invite discussion about emotions and feelings associated with the changing environment?" she asked. "Yes, and the process I'd suggest is similar to what we've done here this morning. This may be different from the way you have conducted business in the past, but times have changed, and it's not business as usual. You're doing business differently than you did in the past, and that calls for new methods for getting work done."

A room full of heads nodded their affirmation. It's sinking in, Stephanie thought.

"Providing the opportunity for your employees to get their feelings out may be their only constructive opportunity to do so," she said. "Oh, sure, they may be talking with their friends, but I would submit to you that those are conversations focused on the 'victim,' who needs to find someone to blame. None of that complaining is focused on finding a positive solution that provides hope for a better future. It only reinforces the 'we're-in-this-together/us-against-them' mentality. The sooner they talk about their feelings in a positive arena, the sooner they'll be able to move on. Of course, you need to have a positive agenda for each meeting, not just allow a bitch session to happen. We all know where those lead."

Again, heads nodded.

"In fact," she went on, "many companies, like mine, bring in an outside facilitator to lead the first couple of sessions for the group. This allows them to become familiar with the exercise and time to develop group facilitation skills. Besides," she added, "using an outsider makes the group more comfortable about revealing their true feelings. They can say what they need to say without fear of it leaking back to management."

4. LEARN ABOUT THE EFFECTS OF SURVIVOR SYNDROME

"On Earth, several authors have written about internal survivors and downsizing. There also is information about downsizing being shared on the Internet, and" — a pause; a grin — "and if you know what you're doing, it's probably easy to find."

The Chiefs chuckled, recalling Stephanie's earlier misadventures on the Web.

"I'd like to suggest," Stephanie continued, "that you read additional material and look for classes that will help build skills to manage your future. Do it now, and start working toward continual improvement."

She hesitated. "I know some of you are thinking, 'When will I find time to read books and attend seminars and prepare for the future when I'm so busy now, I can't finish what I need to because I'm doing the work of two or three people?' Am I right?"

She was answered by sheepish grins.

"I am. I thought so. Well, don't think of learning as a burden. Instead, think of it as additional data you need to be better prepared to make choices about your future. Work it in as you can."

As she finished, she found herself standing next to Pete. "I think that will wrap up our review for this morning," she announced. "How about a 20-minute break? I know some of you need to check in and deal with business. Harry has arranged for refreshments to be served next door in the Galaxy Room, so that's where you'll find drinks and snacks."

☆ ☆ ☆ ☆

As the Chiefs rose to leave the room, Stephanie found herself making a mental note of their body language. Was she getting through to them? Could they see themselves applying this information to what was happening in Virtual Cove? Or did it only apply to employees on Earth? As if they heard her questions, several of the Chiefs stopped by on their way out of the sci-fi auditorium to thank her. Many made a point of telling her how interesting it was that someone from Earth could know what it was like for them in Virtual Cove.

"It's almost like you've been spying on us," commented Les, and smiled.

Stephanie stood, her face frozen in a smile. It was creepy, how they seemed to read her mind. It had happened more than once.

She watched as Les reached the door, turned and smiled at her again.

☆ ☆ ☆ ☆

It wasn't until the last Chief left the room that Stephanie heaved a sigh, fully struck by the force of her adventure. It was only 20 minutes, but it was a much-needed break, she decided. She was looking forward to getting something to drink and finding a quiet spot, away from the others.

Then a hand grabbed her arm.

Stephanie, terrified, swung around with fist clenched and ready to swing. Seeing only Pete, she stopped suddenly and her mind went numb. Only Pete. She felt the red stain that was creeping up her neck and began apologizing profusely.

"Oh, Pete. I'm sorry. You startled me." Her face felt hot. Humiliation, she thought. I feel it and I hate it.

Pete sensed her discomfort. "No, no," he reassured her. "It's all my fault. It *is*," he insisted, over her objections. "You were standing by my chair when you dismissed the group, and I guess you thought everyone was gone. I'm sorry I scared you, especially because I heard about your welcome this morning from Harry. I guess we're not giving you a very favorable impression of Virtual Cove, are we?

"I hope you'll let me make it up to you."

He'd delivered that last comment so casually that Stephanie — for whom there was no longer hope of maintaining composure — felt her face grow hot again. Aware that she was blushing, she silently cursed herself. Stop it, she admonished. You're not a kid.

"How about if I offer you a quiet place in which to put your feet up, and enjoy your coffee and cakes? Would that help make amends for me taking another five years off your life?"

Stephanie wasn't sure what to do. Sure, he was gorgeous — that disarming smile she'd just fielded left no doubt about it. But she couldn't get past how the Chiefs seemed to read her mind. Imagine if he was reading hers now, she thought, hoping with all her heart he wasn't. As tempting as the invitation was, she wasn't sure she was willing to take the risk.

Then again, why not? she rationalized. I'll be gone by tonight.

"I'd be delighted," she heard herself say.

Pete suggested she take a seat in a small room off the auditorium while he went for the coffee and tea cakes. She complied, grateful that she didn't have to go into the break room and subject herself to one-on-one questioning. All she wanted right now was to relax for a few minutes before they got started again. It was going to be a long day and she needed to pace herself.

Pete returned with a tray on which a carafe of coffee, a silver dish filled with unusual cakes, and a beautiful flower in a bud vase were arranged. Stephanie responded with a smile that spread from one dimpled cheek to the next. She was embarrassed; she was impressed.

What is going on with me, she thought.

"I hope you will accept this pampering as an apology for the unfortunate misunderstanding," Pete explained, returning the smile. "I'm really sorry that I scared you."

"Well, it looks like you're on the right track," she grinned.

They were silent for a moment. Then Pete spoke.

"Stephanie?"

"Yes?"

"Come here. Stand next to me, give me your hand, and close your eyes."

Heart fluttering, Stephanie felt her face again grow warm. She wasn't sure what this was all about, but somehow she knew it would be okay. Anyway, this man was not about to go and do something stupid with 20 people in the next room.

So she stood up, moved closer to him, took his hand and closed her eyes, trying to focus on the muted conversation coming from the next room.

Then she heard Pete whisper, "Stephanie? Welcome to my garden."

It was like a thousand violins were playing as she opened her eyes and saw that she was outside — never mind that she had never even moved her feet. Her eyes came to rest on a spectacular view and the violins intensified their serenade. Before her spread a vast meadow of vividly colored flowers, great cornucopias of tissue paper and silk, but real — the billows and folds exuded the scent of gardenia. Stephanie couldn't imagine that they were real; what she wouldn't do to raise these in her garden!

Abandoning her professional persona, Stephanie became a child, a free soul who stood there on the top of a mountain with the world literally at her feet. "Wheeeee!" she squealed, and ran over to Pete, who was seated at a small glass table covered with a beautiful lace cloth.

"How did you do that?" she breathed. "I never even felt my feet move! Where are we? I need to be back in 15 minutes."

Pete sat, sipping coffee flavored with Mandarin orange and basked in her reaction with pure enjoyment. He wasn't ready to tell her that in Virtual Cove, anyone can make real any situation they wish to be in. "I'll explain it to you later," he said. "If you only have 15 minutes, you better sit down, relax, and enjoy your coffee in the quiet of the mountains of Zeplo."

Stephanie, dumbfounded, slowly sank into the chair next to him. She gazed out at the Technicolor flowers, which were swaying trance-like in the warm Spring breeze. The flowers, the sun, the blue sky — all of it seemed so real. Or was it virtual? Wherever this place was, she was sure it was pretty close to Heaven.

☆ ☆ ☆ ☆

As Stephanie returned to the auditorium, the room was abuzz. People were arriving and finding their seats, saying quick hellos to other Chiefs and shuffling through notes. All of the Chiefs had returned for the next part of the session, Stephanie noted, pleased.

"Well, it's three o'clock. I know that many of you have plans for tonight, since this session wasn't scheduled in advance." The group murmured, amused. Stephanie was growing curious about the energy in the room She hoped what was causing it was the resurrection of the image of her Mary Poppins-like arrival. If they were reading her mind, which was recovering with difficulty from the break, she would have to sink into the floor. No question.

She took a deep breath and went on. "I'd like to suggest that since we only have a few more hours together, we decide on two things. One, what time would you like to finish and two, what would feel better for you: Should I abandon my outline so we can explore your thoughts and answer your specific questions?"

Stephanie walked among the Chiefs, hands clasped behind her back. The group seemed to be considering these options when a Chief who had not yet spoken stood.

"Stephanie, my name is Bert Jones. I'm Chief of the Shop-til-you-Drop Satellite Company. I think what we're struggling with is that we'd like to spend more time with you on this Survivor Syndrome/downsizing learning experience. We discussed at break how surprised we are that so much of what you have shared is exactly how we feel. We're concerned that we won't know enough to help ourselves if you leave tonight. So do you think there's any way you could stay for another day or two?"

Stephanie heard the words and she felt the sincerity with which they were said. If she was honest with herself, the opportunity to engage in a symbiotic learn-learn relationship, if even for another day or two, was exciting. She had to admit this was a very intriguing place.

But how could she stay? Where? And what would she wear?

Rita raised her hand. "Stephanie, I'd like to piggyback Bert's comments. This has been so enlightening for me. I would love to continue this discussion until about six tonight and pick up with it again in the morning. I'd be more than glad to have you stay at my flat," she continued. "Virtual Cove has a lot to offer as far as virtual shopping, so don't worry about clothes. Anyway, I'm sure any one of us would do whatever we could to make your stay worthwhile and pleasant.

"Please consider sharing just a little more time with us. Thank you."

Stephanie was overwhelmed, and flattered. How could she refuse?

"Thanks for the offer, Rita. Virtual shopping — that sounds like something I could get used to." Some of the Chiefs clapped as she reached for the laser pad, as if that settled it. "Perhaps I'll decide never to go home." With that, everyone applauded.

LESSON FOUR

What's Driving Downsizing Strategy

Stephanie turned to the group, totally confident among friends. "Okay. Let's just spend a little time talking about why you decided to downsize," she said. "I've heard lots of comments, but we haven't really focused on what drove your decisions. So let's do that now.

"What are some of the reasons your company decided to downsize?" she asked, ready to list them on the wall. Harry told me that you all have the capability to print any of the screens from your seats, so help yourselves to any information we're creating that you'd like to take with you."

75

As Stephanie listened to their stories, the list grew:

☆ COMPETITION

☆ ADVANCED TECHNOLOGY

☆ UNAWARE OF WHAT THE COMPETITION IS DOING

☆ OUR COMPANY MERGED WITH A BIGGER COMPANY

☆ COSTS TOO HIGH

☆ JUST NOT AS MUCH DEMAND FOR OUR PRODUCT
   AS IN THE PAST

☆ NEEDED TO REACT QUICKER TO CUSTOMER
   NEEDS

☆ WE ACQUIRED ANOTHER COMPANY AND HAD TO
   ELIMINATE DUPLICATION

☆ STRUCTURE NEEDED TO BE MORE FLEXIBLE AND
   LESS BUREAUCRATIC SPORADIC WORK VOLUME - -
   WE JUST COULDN'T AFFORD TO KEEP EVERYONE
   ON THE PAYROLL WAITING FOR WORK

☆ ☆ ☆ ☆

As the list accumulated, Stephanie gazed up at it, awestruck. "I can't believe it. This same list could have been generated on Earth by any company in the United States, regardless of industry.

My guess is, you didn't see a downsizing coming. You weren't able to see it until it was too late. When you saw the signs, you assumed it was a cyclical reaction that would pass. Am I right?" She looked around the room and saw that she was. "And perhaps," she continued slowly, "as time passes, you view downsizing more and more as a management prerogative rather than a key business strategy."

They did.

"So we have many things in common between our two worlds. But I think the thing that strikes me most is the fact that our businesses are being run by people — people who have emotions, intuition, pride, egos, reputations and, yes, even commitment to their companies. Or at least they used to."

Stephanie stepped back to the podium to refer to her notes. "When I consider what is happening in corporations in the United States, it's overwhelming. More than 9 million workers permanently lost their jobs between 1991 and 1993. In 1995, almost 440,000 jobs were cut. At the end of June 1996, announced job cuts were up 28% over the same period in 1995.

"I know these numbers are staggering. What's more, the business decisions driving these trends will suffer long-lasting effects. One survey conducted in the United States in 1995 reported that less than half of companies that had implemented a major restructuring believed their companies were more efficient and competitive than they were before the restructuring. Of those firms, only 42 percent of the managers believed their bosses have a clear sense of direction, and only 36 percent felt free to disagree with upper management. Most of these statistics suggested the optimism that had been expressed in a similar survey conducted in 1991, had declined."

As Stephanie surveyed the room, she could see the Chiefs considering the impact of the sobering statistics she was sharing. She imagined they were comparing them to their own numbers in Virtual Cove. "I'm not sharing this to make you feel uncomfortable," she said. "Nor should you feel guilty about your decisions. You did what you had to do for your company to survive. It's just that if this is the road you believe you need to travel, you also must realize not all the effects of the decision will be positive, and attention will need to be paid to the resulting side effects.

"I'm not sure if you have an equivalent system here in Virtual Cove," Stephanie continued, pouring a glass of water, "but back on Earth, Wall Street usually is quick to cheer when a U.S.-based company announces a decision to restructure and downsize. The stockholders usually are assured that their investment will benefit from this effort. The board of directors and executive management team are sure their decision will allow them to achieve the performance and profitability goals they have agreed to. But then," she warned, "something happens."

She sipped her water, put the glass down, and called up a list of statistics she had prepared earlier. They appeared on the screen:

☆ 60 PERCENT OF WORKERS IN DOWNSIZED COMPANIES REPORT AN INCREASE IN THEIR WORKLOADS

- ✩ 156 MILLION WORK DAYS ARE LOST EVERY YEAR TO DEPRESSION, SOME OF IT CAUSED BY THE WAY WORKERS ARE TREATED BY SUPERVISORS AND MANAGEMENT

- ✩ 75 PERCENT OF WORKERS FEEL COMPANIES ARE LESS LOYAL TO WORKERS

- ✩ 53 PERCENT OF WORKERS SAY THE MOOD AT WORK IS ANGRIER THAN IT WAS IN PREVIOUS YEARS

- ✩ 69 PERCENT OF EXECUTIVES SURVEYED ADMITTED THEY HAD SENT OUT RESUMES

- ✩ SURVIVORS SUFFER FROM GREATER STRESS, BURNOUT, ANXIETY, ANGER, INSECURITY AND CYNICISM

Stephanie's eyes met theirs. Something told her they already knew some of this.

LESSON FIVE

Minimizing the Effects of Negative Emotions and Behaviors

This would prove to be Stephanie's favorite part of the presentation. "When addressing the emotions employees feel when the threat of losing their job is a possibility, I like to compare it to the emotions people exhibit when they lose a loved one," she said, clicking on the computerized chart-maker and prompting the model to appear:

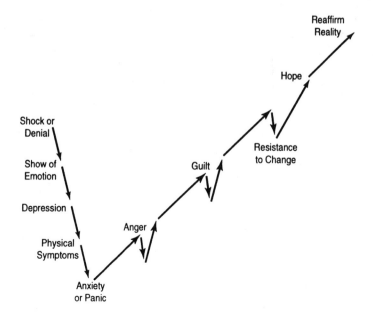

"Remember what I said earlier?" she asked. "The loss of a job is second on the list of the stressful events people experience in their lifetimes. The first is the loss of a loved one and the emotions are very, very similar. How many of you have experienced the loss of someone close to you? Fewer than half of the Chiefs raised their hands. Pete was among them. "Well, this model," she continued pointing to the screen, "can help you identify what emotions you are likely to see in yourself, or in your co-workers and employees."

Stephanie then called attention to the chart (Figure 3) that displayed the range of emotions: denial, depression, anxiety, anger, guilt, hope — and, finally, the acknowledgment of reality and acceptance for what is. When she was finished with her overview, she noticed that someone in the audience had raised his hand.

Pete.

"Pete? Did you have something you'd like to add?"

Pete stood. "Well, as most of the folks in this room know, I lost my wife two years ago in a galactic crash. It was freak accident. It wasn't supposed to happen and an accident like that has not happened since, but the fact is, she died. We had been married 27 years. When I look at that chart I remember the many emotions I went through, but I didn't go through them one at a time. It was more like I was traveling in a space-ship out of control — sometimes going forward, sometimes backwards, and at times I felt I was flying upside down. How does that play into your chart, or was my experience just unusual?"

Stephanie found herself trying to imagine what his wife looked like and how they acted together. From what she had observed of Pete, he was a kind, gentle and caring person. She imagined his wife was just as lovely.

"Thank you for sharing your experience, Pete, and for bringing up such an important point. You're right. Employees confronted by significant change in the work environment will feel like they're on a rollercoaster or, as you said, in a spaceship.

Pointing to the model, she continued, "the important thing to remember is that your movement through these emotions is not linear. Just as Pete described, you can be in denial one moment and depression the next, and back to anger after that. And the thing that makes what you're dealing with so difficult is that you are switching your emotions as different situations present themselves. This can be as frequent as minute to minute, hour to hour, or day to day.

"What makes this even more complex," she said, studying Pete's blue eyes for a reaction, "is that each and every one of your employees also is on his or her own emotional trip in his or her own spaceship. You don't travel through this as one big group. It's more like looking at the stars in the sky at night. Every star has its own spot, and its own brightness. Some are traveling fast and others are slow. I hope, as you and your co-workers travel at your own speeds, there will be a point in time when you find yourselves at acceptance.

"But it also is important to realize that not all of you or all of your co-workers will get to this point," she warned, walking among the tables. "You or a co-worker may have had an event in your life that will permanently prevent you from accepting the type of change going on at work. Or perhaps your employees have developed perceptions about how things are being handled by the company that are just too hurtful to forgive. Or perhaps you or your co-workers have other changes going on in your life that have absorbed all the energy you have to deal with change, and there is no more energy to draw from. All kinds of things will influence the speed at which individuals arrive at acceptance. The important thing to remember is that the feelings of each and every individual, including your feelings, are legitimate emotions. So even if you could never imagine yourself experiencing a particular emotion that someone else is struggling with, don't belittle it. If they say that's what they are feeling, it's real — at least for them."

Silence.

☆ ☆ ☆ ☆

"Because this is so important," Stephanie continued, pacing among the work tables, "let's spend a little time talking about these emotions in more detail. The information I'm about to present is not from my personal research. The model we've been looking at was developed by Granger Westburg, who holds a joint professorship in medicine and religion at the University of Chicago and a professorship in preventative medicine at the University of Illinois College of Medicine." With that, the model (figure 5) appeared on the wall.

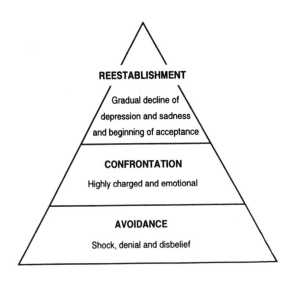

REESTABLISHMENT
Gradual decline of
depression and sadness
and beginning of acceptance

CONFRONTATION
Highly charged and emotional

AVOIDANCE
Shock, denial and disbelief

"I'm also going to refer to the work of Therese Rando, Ph.D., as we look further at how employees respond to loss. If you want more information about emotions people go through when dealing with significant loss, you might also want to research some of the work developed by Elizabeth Kubler Ross."

Stephanie arrived at the front of the auditorium and turned to face the Chiefs. "I want you to understand these emotions because, although you may not personally experience all of them, you need to be aware and sensitive to the feelings that others will be dealing with on their transition journeys.

"Usually, when employees hear about a downsizing, or a merger, or the possibility of any of this happening, they just don't believe it. This kind of news is especially hard to believe if the organization has been around for many years and has had a relatively stable history."

Stephanie began writing on her laser tablet:

AVOIDANCE, SHOCK, DENIAL & DISBELIEF

☆ "I CAN'T BELIEVE THEY WOULD DO THIS."

☆ "I'LL JUST WAIT. YOU'LL SEE, EVERYTHING WILL GO BACK TO NORMAL."

As the words appeared on the wall, she again turned to the group. "How many of you have felt these emotions, or know someone in your organization who has?"

Rita's hand was the first to go up. "I'm not sure we're not still in denial, but many of my employees, and I have to say myself included, can still be heard saying things like, 'When they come to their senses, we'll go back to treating people the way we used to.' What I find paralyzing about that attitude, at least for me, is that waiting for things to go back to the old way robs us of the chance to work in the new way."

Stephanie was about to comment when another Chief responded. "What's ironic to me is, in an industry that has never relied on the past, but instead always pushed the envelope looking for what was new and creative, we have become stuck. It's like someone has painted a circle around us and forbade us to cross the line.

"What are we afraid of?" he asked.

Stephanie had moved from the platform stage to stand next to him. Looking around the room, she said, "Don't ever underestimate the power of the human mind. Why would you or one of your co-workers want to invest time and energy integrating new practices if you felt it was just a matter of time before things returned to the way they were? If employees only hear about changes and don't see them, why should they believe that it's anything but words?"

84

Then, turning her attention back to the Chief who had spoken, "I can picture you and your employees standing clustered in a circle drawn with a wide, white line. That's exactly how some employees feel. If they cross the line, they may be expected to learn different tasks, take care of themselves in a different way than they did before, become empowered and accountable for their actions and yes, maybe they will even have to look for new employment. All of those things are scary and take courage to face. But once the individual faces her fears, she realizes she can make a positive contribution to any employer, not just her current one. She learns she has options she wasn't aware of before."

☆ ☆ ☆ ☆

Stephanie again moved back to the stage. "As individuals try to deal with the shock of the news — that the organization is downsizing — they also may go through another emotion: confrontation. At this stage, the employee finds herself emotionally charged with an extreme sense of violation. In many industries on Earth, violence in the workplace is increasing. Some of that is attributed to the emotions employees experience during this phase of grieving."

Leaning on the podium, Stephanie continued, "Remember earlier today, when we were talking about the importance of emotional release? This is another reason to allow yourself and others to express your feelings out loud. If individuals are denied that opportunity, those feelings will surface in some other manner at some other time. Unfortunately, for some, it surfaces as anger in dealing with co-workers, short tempers with clients, or violent acts in the workplace or at home."

As Stephanie finished writing CONFRONTATION on the tablet, Pete stood up. "If it's okay with you, Stephanie, I'd like to give an example of something I've seen and get your comments about how I can deal with it."

Stephanie assented.

"Well," he began, "I have an assistant chief who's never had to fire anybody. He's been with our organization for about 10 years and is a great contributor. He made it very clear when I first announced the downsizing that he felt betrayed. He thought he would be with our company for the rest of his career, and was furious that we had 'changed the rules on him,' as he put it.

"This fellow is a good leader and a good worker. I don't want to lose him, but I feel like he's never going to get over the emotional impact of this decision. As I'm listening to you speak, I'm wondering how many others have employees who feel betrayed, and what are you doing about it?"

Then Harry rose. He had been quiet most of the day, but he had taken copious notes. Stephanie had wondered how long he could contain himself.

"Yes, Harry? What would you like to add?"

"I too have seen and heard from employees who have acted as if they have been attacked by their best friend. They're shocked. They can't believe it's happening. They can't imagine life without performing *that* specific job in our company. My company is trying to help them see the value of their skills and experience through career-management workshops, so that they won't dread looking for a job elsewhere, if it comes to that.

"But they keep resisting me. They ask how I can understand what they're feeling when I'm not at risk of losing my job. They just don't trust me." He paused. "And as Stephanie knows, today, for the first time in the history of my company, an employee brought a laser gun to work!" This announcement was greeted by murmurs of shock and surprise.

"We didn't even have a policy in place for something like that, because we never thought about it happening," he continued. "So like Pete, I'm wondering how can I help myself and my employees. I'd like to be proof that there's hope."

Stephanie went to Harry. "I'm sorry I don't have an answer that will always provide hope to your employees. All I can tell you is that you need to have patience and just stay focused on the issues we have been discussing. None of what we're talking about today is a quick fix — there are none. You need to be honest with yourself and your employees, and demonstrate commitment to the new behaviors you're looking for so that employees know you are serious.

"Something we've already mentioned might also be helpful to try. Allow your employees to talk about the emotions they're feeling. Perhaps they can't talk about it at home with their families. Perhaps they interpret what is happening as a statement of their competency. Not only are they viewing the organization as a traitor, they also may be doubting what work they are capable of performing. As they talk openly about these issues, there is one important thing for you to remember: It takes time for the heart to heal, and after it does there will always be a scar. However, by giving them the right skills, and the time to get comfortable with their own intuition about their skills and their passions, they will be able to deliver hope to themselves. They won't have to depend on the company or anyone else for it."

Stephanie glanced at her notes. "I guess what I'm trying to say is, the relationship will never be the same as it was. Expect anger, expect mistrust and expect that it will take time to accept what is happening and react positively. Help employees get counseling through employee assistance programs, and provide opportunities to discover their feelings by introducing interventions much like those we have practiced this morning. They don't really trust you or your intentions, so this may be difficult at first. But don't give up.

"We'll talk about this later," she continued, "but let me mention now that you should also consider that some of your managers or assistants may not be ready to facilitate discussion of emotions. In fact, some of you may determine that your interpersonal skills also need improvement. In the short term, you may want to use resources outside your firm. For the long run, it would be a good investment to offer managers and team leaders the chance to improve their facilitation, coaching and listening skills."

☆ ☆ ☆ ☆

Stephanie glanced at her watch. It was getting close to six. "Wow," she remarked. "The afternoon has gone by so quickly. I'd like to finish up our discussion about emotions and call it a day. How does that sound to you?"

As self-appointed group spokesman, Harry moved to the front of the room and turned to face the audience. "This morning," he declared, "this delightful young woman landed in our Cove. She had no idea what was happening to her. I very ungraciously scared her to death and hours later, here she is, generously sharing so much information that it's making my head spin.

"I think it would be prudent to complete this session and call it a night. We'll meet back here tomorrow morning at nine to finish up. I can only speak for myself, but I know there are several things that I'm anxious to discuss with my managers." Turning to Stephanie, he said, "I again publicly apologize for this morning and thank you for agreeing to talk to us. Your staying one more day is delightful. I promise, you'll be back in your office tomorrow."

The room broke out in applause. Stephanie, ears pink, was touched by the connection she felt with her new friends. "Thank you, Harry," she said, and crossed the platform to finish up business.

"Now, how about we look at the last phase of grief?" Strawberry blonde head bent over the tablet, she began to write:

RE-ESTABLISHMENT: GRADUAL DECLINE
OF DENIAL AND THE BEGINNING OF
ACCEPTANCE

"From what I've heard, not many of you have seen a lot of acceptance. But there are some things that go on prior to acceptance that, perhaps, you are seeing. If so, you're probably wondering how it fits in with this emotional transition." Stephanie was about to pour another glass of water, but opted instead for a glass pitcher that contained some sort of ruby-colored liquid. She took a sip; sensed on her upper lip something akin to cherry cordial and pineapple. "Pleasant," she observed, to no one.

Then she continued. "For employees to get to the acceptance part of it, they're going to have to experiment with the change and learn how to remove barriers holding them back. As I said, they're going to have to talk about it, explore their own emotions, and do some work around inner reflection. They're going to have to work through their anger, and they'll have to adjust to a culture that has shifted from one of dependence on the company to independence from the company.

"As each employee travels this road to the future, there will be many perilous moments. One would be realizing that they're required to manage their own careers, or figure out what training and new skills they'll need to keep abreast of their profession. Those were things the organization used to take the lead on, but it can't afford to do that anymore.

"Of course, they may need help with this, some more than others. There will be times that won't be comfortable. At first, they may need help figuring out a plan for attending workshops, reading new materials, visiting different Web site. or participating in support groups comprised of similar employees. Then there comes a day when someone says something like, 'I'm interested in taking a class that will broaden my knowledge.' Or, 'I didn't ask your opinion about this decision, because I understand that you're here to empower me to take care of this.' You'll see how it's all making a difference.

Stephanie paused. "Sometimes, they need to get comfortable with what's happening by feeling confident about what they have to offer. The realization may sound like, 'I've put my resume together, and I amazed myself with the knowledge and skills I've accumulated over the past 15 years. I'd really like to stay, but if that's not in the cards, I know I can be valuable to another firm.'

"I know this may be a little premature, but have any of you heard these kinds of statements?"

This time a middle-aged man sitting at the back of the room raised his hand. Stephanie had been watching him all day. He didn't seem to want to participate actively — he seemed to want to just listen. Previous experience had taught her that some employees come to participate passively; she had concluded that this man had come to do just that. She knew he would open up when he was ready. Apparently, that moment had come.

"My name is Juan," he said, standing to address the group. Juan's tall frame was swathed in clothing that was very casual: tan Chinos, soft maroon polo shirt and a pair of loafers. "I've been listening to all of you, all day. When I decided to take Harry up on his offer, I wasn't sure what to expect. I sure wasn't thinking we'd be talking about feelings and communications and strategies for helping ourselves and others. Heck," he laughed, "I just didn't know what to expect." The audience chuckled and several heads nodded in agreement.

"Anyway," Juan continued, "I'm sitting here listening and all of a sudden I have this urge to share a few observations of my own. So I hope you will allow me a few minutes to get them out."

He paused, half expecting someone to object.

"I haven't necessarily heard any of my employees make the statements that Stephanie mentioned, but I've been hearing employees at my manufacturing plant say things like, 'I want to do something to regain control over my destiny,' or, 'When I get over this, I'm never gonna let a company own me again.'

"I know that's not exactly what you've been saying, but I sense that these employees are healing themselves somehow and are getting ready to accept a different future. Now I know they can't rely on the company to make all their decisions, and I guess I also know I don't want them to. But if they are getting ready for acceptance, how do they accept what is happening and also have some kind of loyalty to the firm and their work?"

"Those are excellent examples," Stephanie chimed in. "Tell me, Juan, what kind of business do you have?"

"I own the largest spacecraft manufacturing plant this side of Earth," he said, proudly. " Most of the ships you'll see jetting around out here were designed, manufactured, assembled and distributed by my company. Our headquarters are here in Virtual Cove."

Stephanie considered this. "Your comments describe people in movement and people working through anger," she replied. "They sound like they're beginning to believe that things have changed, that their job stability may never be the way it once was. However, they're not quite sure they can believe it 100 percent. At this stage, employees are dealing with how they fit in, and wondering which skills and talents they possess that might still be needed by the company. They're watching how other employees are being treated — both those being let go and those staying — to determine if this new environment suits their beliefs and values about how people should be treated. They're experimenting with spreading their wings, and making plans that will allow them to strengthen those wings so that when they need to fly, they're ready."

Stephanie had again gravitated toward Pete's table. "Remember," she said, "it takes time to work one's way to acceptance. What is critical for the organization is to be ready for it. Support employees. Encourage them to be more independent in their work habits and with their future plans. You can provide them with the tools and training to pursue self-managed career development. Encourage them to pursue continuous learning, as it's vital to their future, and give them an environment that supports open, honest communication about the current business climate and what can be expected in the future. This is the perfect time to ensure that your procedures and policies reward risk-takers, and that failures are examined for lessons to be learned. They'll appreciate open communication about the skills believed critical for workers-of-the-future."

Stephanie, organizing her next thought, moved to the back of the room to stand next to Juan's table. "There's only one thing I'm sorry to say," she said, looking directly at him. "You need to know that they will never feel the same way about the company, their job or you. Like I said, things will never be the same for employees being let go; nor will it be the same for those who remain. That's why it's so important to pay some attention to those employees who are staying. How can they possibly take your company into a successful future if they are in shock, if they don't know how they fit, and if they're not sure who to trust?

"By spending some time with them, they will come to learn to assess their skills and take control of their own destiny. They'll also feel good about your support and the fact that you care about their futures, even if they do have to make things happen for themselves. And they'll figure out how to accept and change to function in the new environment by watching the behaviors that you and your managers model every day.

"I want to make something very clear, though," she warned, heading back to the podium. "I don't want to mislead you. Regardless of what you do, you will not be able to recreate the loyalty you enjoyed in the past. The 'loyalty,' if we can use that word, created in the new relationship will stem from respectful appreciation that you care enough to help them to be employable, not just employed. In exchange for that respect, they'll give you a good day's work."

☆ ☆ ☆ ☆

MAKING A NEW FRIEND

Harry stood and joined her on the stage as Stephanie was saying, "It appears we need to wrap this discussion up for the evening. I really appreciate this opportunity. Actually, I'm amazed at how much I've learned from you and the ideas you have given me for making changes at my company in Atlanta. I know I'll be a more open and sensitive manager when I return, thanks to your stories.

"If there aren't any more questions, we'll call it a day. I hope to see you all tomorrow morning around nine. Have a good evening."

As the room began to clear, Harry once again asked Stephanie if she would be okay for the evening. "No problem," she cheerfully replied. "You go ahead with your plans. Rita has graciously offered to put me up for the evening and, to tell you the truth, I can't wait to see what the night life is like out here among the stars."

"All right, then," Harry smiled, packing up his notes. As he started down the platform steps, he turned to her and called, "I'll see you in the morning."

Stephanie returned to collecting her notes and straightening up her work area. Soon the sound of high-heeled boots clicking across the smooth stone floor announced Rita's approach. Thank goodness she didn't forget me, Stephanie thought, shuffling the day's notes into a semi-neat stack and placing it on the podium. I don't know what I would have done if she had.

Rita, dark curls bouncing on the shoulders of her cherry red bolero, appeared and Stephanie immediately sensed a problem. Rita's forehead was furrowed by a frown that marked the otherwise placid features.

"Stephanie," she began. "Oh, Stephanie. I'm so sorry. I can't believe what has happened. I'm not going to be able to take you home with me this evening." The words tumbled out in a rush. "My family is on a trip out of town and I have to meet up with them because my husband has taken ill. I just got an intergalactic message as you were closing the session and when I tuned in, it was my daughter saying that Paul, my husband, had been rushed to the clinic for treatment. I'm really sorry to leave you in a lurch, but I've got to run."

Stephanie's mind was already racing over her options. Finding none when she realized she had neglected to get a phone number from Harry, her concern was not helped by Rita's plight. Naturally, she didn't want to make her feel worse than she already did, so Stephanie tried to reassure her.

"Really, Rita, it's okay. Don't worry! Go to your family and don't worry about me. I'm quite the traveler, remember," she smiled, referring to her morning trip. "I'll do just fine. Anyway, there are hotels in Virtual Cove, aren't there?"

There were. "Thanks for understanding," Rita said, returning the smile apologetically. "I'll definitely try to make it to tomorrow's session." Thrusting her hands into the pockets of her mini-length leather skirt, she nodded a quick good-bye, turned, and hurried away, the click-click of her boots fading away in the hall.

Silence took over, and Stephanie had never felt so alone.

☆ ☆ ☆ ☆

Stephanie was wondering about finding a place to stay and a place to eat, but she also couldn't help but feel cheated out of experiencing first-hand the cyberspace night life. She also was sorry that Rita was not going to be available for the evening. She liked her.

She resigned herself to the fact that somehow, some-where, this night would be devoted to rest. She had just about convinced herself that this was best when Pete appeared in the doorway. She was surprised to see him.

"I was just about ready to blast off for the evening when I ran into Rita. She told me about her husband, and how badly she felt because she had to abandon you. I thought I'd come back and offer to help you get settled for the evening. That is, if you need help," he added, a little uncertainly.

Stephanie studied him. There he was, leaning against the door frame, thumbs tucked into his belt loops and looking for all the world like a GQ kind of guy. He had unbuttoned his shirt at the collar and dispensed with the flannel blazer entirely. Stephanie carefully examined his kind face and con-cluded that he probably was in his early fifties.

She had dated several men since her divorce, but there just never seemed to be the chemistry she wanted. That she wanted to be with this man caught her off guard. It figures, she thought. I finally meet a man and feel the sparks, and he's in another galaxy!

She cleared her throat. "Well, to tell you the truth, I was just feeling a little sorry for myself, wondering how I'd find my way. I certainly would appreciate you pointing me in the right direction for a nice dinner and a comfortable hotel." She was embarrassed, acutely aware that she sounded like a damsel in distress. I can't help it, she told herself. That's what I feel like.

"I can do better than that, if you're up for company. Do you think you could stand spending a few more hours with one of your students? I promise I'll keep shop talk to a mini-mum," he wheedled, reaching for her notes as though he fully expected her to agree to it.

When she did, he was barely able to mask his delight. Somehow, Stephanie knew he was thinking the same thing she was. This was the kind of beginning that would titillate any enthusiast of storybook romances.

☆ ☆ ☆ ☆

The duo decided to stop by Pete's place to recuperate from the day before stepping out into the evening. Just as he had done on break, Pete stood close to Stephanie, and requested that she close her eyes and hold his hand. She grasped his fingers and felt that she never wanted to let go. She felt safe; she trusted him. And she found herself wanting to know him better.

It was as though Pete sensed she was fantasizing about something terrific — he gently squeezed her hand before he told her to open her eyes. Stephanie, blushing, did, and instantly forgot her embarrassment.

"Wow," she breathed. They were standing on a wide, white verandah. Before her lay an expanse of turquoise sea, its glass surface interrupted only by the occasional playful porpoise that shot straight up from the depths and sailed into the sky, forming a perfect arc against the brilliant cerulean sky. A row of purple windmills stood like stalks on the horizon, blades spinning furiously in tandem; the beach was not like any beach she had ever seen — replacing what traditionally, anyway, was sand was a carpet of multicolored flowers, the same varieties that had delighted her that afternoon.

"Welcome to my home," Pete said, his voice low. "I thought you might like this view after I saw your reaction to the one from this afternoon."

He motioned for her to relax in a sumptuous, soft arm-chair, covered in damask and situated next to a water garden. That such furniture would attend an outdoor setting struck her as odd, but only for a moment — her attention was seized by the pond at the base of the waterfall. Plump water lilies floated peacefully on its surface while, deep within the slate-colored water, bright orange Koi darted and swam.

She couldn't speak.

"I love this spot," he went on. "Especially after a long day, or night, at the office."

They were quiet for a moment. Then Stephanie gazed into his eyes, blue as cornflowers, and cleared her throat. She hoped she had recovered sufficiently from her awe to at least say something.

"Pete," she began, relieved to hear her voice behaving itself. "How did I get here?"

The explanation was highly technical. Though interested, Stephanie was distracted by her surroundings. *Alice in Wonderland*, she thought. Lewis Carroll would have loved this. She heard Pete's voice, but was unable to follow the words. Concentration was impossible in the face of what lay before her.

"...travel, therefore, is divided into 'microunits.' We don't say 'miles per hour.' Oh, we do, or at least those who are Earth natives do, but it doesn't really apply here."

Finished, Pete was again silent, and Stephanie felt a little awkward. Something told her it wasn't a comfortable silence. She bit her lip, wondering what, if anything, she had done to cause it.

Finally, she cleared her throat again and ventured, "I don't know you very well, I know. But have I done something to make you uncomfortable? You don't seem to be as relaxed as when we landed here."

This time it was Pete's turn to be embarrassed. "I was so looking forward to rescuing you and spending the evening with you," he blurted. "Now that you're here, I'm very self-conscious about the fact that we're here alone. I mean, you don't know where you are, or how to get back.

"So I guess I just want you to know that I'm very trustworthy and my intentions are honorable. If you're at all uncomfortable, we can concoct a chaperone. I won't be offended," he finished with a deep breath, glad to get that off his chest.

Stephanie smiled and took his hand. "All of what you've said is definitely true," she said. "But to be quite honest with you, I feel that somehow I've known you for a long time. I feel that I can trust you and have not had any thoughts about intentions that were anything but aboveboard. I guess I'm looking at this as an adventure and you're my tour guide.

"Please, don't worry about me. I'll let you know if this adventure gets uncomfortable. Anyway, this is *your* home. You shouldn't be tense. It's going to be a fun evening, you know." She smiled as their fingers intertwined.

"Good," he smiled back. "Now that that's out of the way, let me show you the house and point you in the direction of the computer so you can get yourself refreshed for the evening."

They rose; Pete ushered her through the door and into the mansion. As she went, Stephanie looked around, trying to take in everything at once and wondering what new technology she would find.

"I can't believe what you have available at your fingertips," she declared as they descended the stairs into what appeared to be an entertainment room. "This is better than those arcades full of video games. There you get to try and shoot some hyperactive little icon that jumps and runs all over the place. This is using technology for real," she observed, marveling at strange-looking machines in assorted colors and sizes. Each was studded with rows of buttons that permitted almost every household activity to be performed simply by pushing the right ones. It's like the Jetsons, she thought.

Pete left her alone in the huge guest suite after he had concluded the tour of the house and provided her with minimal instructions on using the Virtual Shopping Network. It took very little time for her to get used to the gentle massage and relaxation sessions that began with the click of a mouse - - in moments she felt completely refreshed, as though she'd slept for nine hours. Nor could she find fault with the Virtual Shopping Network. Just order it, and it appears. She happened to think she looked pretty good in her new cyberspace jumpsuit, and Pete's expression when she reappeared wearing it confirmed her suspicions." That's one of the lovely advantages of living in Virtual Cove," he remarked, regarding her intently. "Everything is at your fingertips. Speaking of that, can I interest you in a glass of wine before dinner?"

He could, though both her head and her spirit were already light.

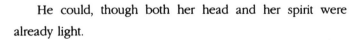

☆ ☆ ☆ ☆

The wine was delicious so as to defy description. (Later, Stephanie would try to locate it on Earth, telling the puzzled clerk that all she knew was that it tasted of some combination of plumbs, butterscotch and fallen leaves.) As they sipped,

Pete announced dinner options. The bottom line, he said, is that "you can have anything your little heart desires."

Stephanie described what she thought would be a nice evening, trying to not make it sound too romantic. When they finished, Pete again took her hand, and they were off.

During dinner, Pete wanted to know all about Stephanie. He was curious about everything. What was she like as a child? Where did she grow up? Where did she go to college? How did she like working in communications?

When she had answered what seemed like the 500th question, she asked, "With all this technology available, isn't there any way for you to virtually research me and know everything you want to know?"

Pete smiled. "Now you're catching on," he said. "And yes. That technology is available. But Stephanie, I must be honest with you. I'm having a much better time listening to you tell the story than I would if my computer told it." With that, they laughed and toasted their new friendship.

The evening went by quickly. Pete showed Stephanie around the Cove and they blasted off to a few star-gazing spots. Stephanie had never experienced a night sky like this. The stars were like huge uncut diamonds dancing on a skirt of black velvet. And every once in a while one of the diamonds would burst like a Fourth of July fireworks and propel itself across the sky, leaving a tail that blazed and sparkled as if it had been sprinkled with glitter. Stephanie couldn't help feeling as though she could reach out and pick one of the stars to take home as a souvenir. How sad that they were well beyond her reach, she thought.

"This is like being in Heaven," she observed aloud, leaning against Pete's strong shoulder and half attempting to count the stars in the sky. "You know, back on Earth, these stars and planets look so small. And there you can't see how quickly they're moving. Here, it's as if it's not real."

"Oh, it's real all right," Pete assured her. "But I know what you mean. I've been here almost 30 years now and I'm still amazed when I find a spot like this. I've never brought anyone from Earth here, though — not someone who is experiencing this for the first time. I can only thank you from the bottom of my heart for giving me the opportunity to see this again through your eyes." As he finished, he leaned over and lightly kissed Stephanie's cheek.

"Well, this has all been wonderful," she breathed, face flushed. "In fact, it's been so wonderful that I feel like I need to pinch myself to make sure I'm not dreaming."

"I have a better way of letting you know you're not dreaming," he whispered, as he leaned over and kissed her. It was a long, deep kiss, something they both had wanted all evening. And it was fantastic.

☆ ☆ ☆ ☆

Morning came too quickly. Stephanie, fresh from another bout of virtual shopping, arrived in the kitchen looking like she had just stepped out of the pages of a futuristic Web site. She had.

It didn't take Pete long to notice. "I see you didn't have any trouble with my instructions about shopping," he said, a small grin on his face. As Stephanie ordered up a cup of coffee and a Danish-looking breakfast roll from the computer, she returned the playful chatter.

"Now you don't think a woman of my intelligence would have trouble following directions, do you?"

Pete laughed. Then they moved out to the verandah to enjoy their breakfast.

When they were ready to leave for Virtual Travel's headquarters, Stephanie knew what to do. She stood next to Pete and held out her hand. As he put his hand in hers, she squeezed it. Looking straight into his blue eyes, she said, "I really appreciate your hospitality, Pete. I wasn't sure what to expect of Virtual Cove and of you, and you made me feel very welcome. I hope I get the chance to return the favor some day."

Pete grinned, thrilled with the way things had gone. He was glad that he had taken the risk to invite Stephanie to his home. Yet here in the light of day, he felt exposed, a little vulnerable. So cautiously he replied, "Stephanie, believe me: The pleasure was all mine. It was so much fun to have you visit me and allow me to explore things — things I had come to take for granted — through a fresh pair of eyes."

At this, her face lit up. Feeling encouraged, he continued, "Any time you need a place to stay in Virtual Cove, my door is always open."

That said, he hugged her and they were off.

☆ ☆ ☆ ☆

LESSON SIX

Benefiting from the Changing
Employment Relationship

As Stephanie was preparing her material, the auditorium began to fill. She was glad to see that everyone had again returned. By nine, they were ready to start.

"Let's talk about where we ended yesterday," she began. "Who can tell me some of the emotions and feelings employees go through when the threat of job loss is a possibility?"

"Denial," a Chief shouted.

"Shock," added another.

"Depression, and anger."

"Guilt."

"Acceptance!"

"Good, you *were* listening," Stephanie said with a smile that showed off her dimple. "You're ready to go on.

"This morning we're going to talk about the need for a new employment relationship. Remember yesterday how we discussed the end of the psychological contract?" Heads bobbed in affirmation. "If you think about it, the loyalty, dedication and commitment your employees used to show was done in large part because they wanted to secure their jobs and financial futures. However, along the way it developed into a type of dependency — a dependency we now realize was not healthy. They learned to depend on the company for job stability, annual raises, confirmation of their worth, direction for professional development and, in many cases, social interaction.

"Your employees probably would want your organization to continue most of that. But on the other hand, because of the circumstances we discussed yesterday and the impact of Survivor Syndrome, they're filled with fear, mistrust of management, anger toward the company and little hope for the future. They're suffering from various levels of paralysis, knowing they need to do something to prepare for the future, but feeling so violated and overwhelmed they don't know where to start. It's because of these mixed feelings and emotions that your job — finding the right balance for the new relationship — just became harder."

Descending into the audience, Stephanie looked out at the group and continued. "How do you motivate employees who know they no longer can count on lifetime employment, even if they are dedicated and productive? What incentives can you offer that will create and cement a new employment contract, one to replace the dead psychological contract?"

She was answered by blank stares. "Any ideas?" she repeated, moving among the group. Finally, she stopped and stood next to Pete.

"As my questions appear to have stumped you, let's work on this in small groups and then come together to discuss it." She continued to stroll around the room. "Take the next 15 minutes and discuss these questions with your colleagues. Believe me, effectively battling Survivor Syndrome, and finding the formula for the new employment relationship that allows you to successfully meet the goals of the surviving organization, depends on the creativity of your answers."

She moved to the podium, picked up the laser tablet and wrote:

1   HOW DO YOU MOTIVATE EMPLOYEES WHO ARE NOT GUARANTEED LIFETIME EMPLOYMENT?

2   WHAT INCENTIVES DO YOU OFFER EMPLOYEES TO GET THEM TO HELP CREATE A NEW EMPLOYMENT RELATIONSHIP?

Stephanie looked up at her audience. "As you think about possible solutions, don't be restricted by time, money or talents. Appoint someone at your table to take notes so you can share your ideas with all of us. Any questions?"

106

With a few minutes to relax, Stephanie sat down and observed the groups. Initially, they appeared stumped, but as some stumbled on possible solutions, their excitement grew and they busily began to come up with more options. As they worked, Stephanie thought about the opportunity she would have later in the day to speak to some of the employees of the companies represented at the meeting.

She also thought about the trip she would soon be taking home. To her surprise, those thoughts were somewhat bittersweet. True, she was excited about going back. It's always good to be back at one's own home, and anyway, her impromptu trip had inspired her to consider initiating some new changes at work to aid the remaining employees. But she also had had a lot of fun here, and she felt a little sad.

Reality shook her from her reverie when Harry, suddenly standing next to her, called her name. "Stephanie? Stephanie, are you all right?"

"Oh. Yes. Yes, Harry, I'm fine," she responded, jolted back to the present. "I was just daydreaming."

"Well, I just wanted to seize this opportunity to let you know that, whenever you're ready to go this afternoon, I'll see that you get home. I'm a man of my word and a deal is a deal."

Stephanie smiled up at him, grateful for his help. She would be ready to go at about four, she told him, right after the meeting he had arranged with the employees. As Harry returned to his seat, she stood and asked if anyone needed more time.

"We're ready," shouted Les, adding, "this was the most difficult task you've asked us to do so far. I can't wait to see what everyone else came up with."

Stephanie smiled. "You're right, Les. It is difficult, and I too am eager to hear from the others. Who wants to go first?"

Bert stood. "Before I begin, we'd like to say that we also struggled with this assignment. It's hard to think of the relationship in terms different from the way it currently is.

"The approach we took was twofold. First, we listed what we, the employers, want. Here's what we came up with." Bert walked to the stage. Soon, his list appeared on the big screen:

WHAT EMPLOYERS WANT

☆ SELF-MOTIVATED EMPLOYEES

☆ RISK-TAKERS UNAFRAID OF FAILURE

☆ WORK FORCE THAT UNDERSTANDS TODAY'S BUSINESS PRESSURES

☆ HIGHLY TRAINED STAFF

☆ EMPLOYEES INTERESTED IN CONTINUOUS LEARNING

☆ EMPLOYEES WHO ACCEPT THE FLEXIBLE
NATURE OF WORK AND ARE COMMITTED,
HOWEVER LONG THEY ARE WITH US

☆ WILLING TO GIVE WHATEVER IT TAKES TO DO IT
RIGHT THE FIRST TIME

☆ CUSTOMER-FOCUSED EMPLOYEES

"As you can see, we're expecting a lot," he remarked.

"Then we looked at what we thought the employees want
and this is what we came up with." Another list appeared on
the wall, next to the first:

WHAT EMPLOYEES WANT

☆ BE TRAINED AND PREPARED FOR THE FUTURE

☆ UNDERSTAND WHAT THE CHANGING WORK ENVI-
RONMENT MEANS FOR US

☆ HAVE ROLES, RESPONSIBILITIES AND EXPECTA-
TIONS DEFINED

☆ BE TREATED WITH RESPECT AND DIGNITY

☆ HAVE BENEFITS THAT ARE PORTABLE (CAN
MOVE WITH THEM FROM JOB TO JOB)

☆ RECEIVE HELP ACCEPTING AND ADAPTING TO
THE CHANGING WORK CULTURE

☆ ASSISTANCE WITH BALANCING WORK AND FAM-
ILY

☆ ENLIGHTENED MANAGEMENT STAFF TRAINED IN
COACHING AND FEEDBACK

☆ THE OPPORTUNITY AND SUPPORT TO ENABLE
OURSELVES TO TAKE CHARGE OF OUR OWN
DESTINIES

108

The room erupted in a round of applause. "Don't get too
excited," Bert warned, motioning for them to control their
applause. "We did come up with these two lists, but that's
where we got stuck. Where do we take this? Perhaps one of
the other groups knows what to do from this point?"

Having posed the challenge, Bert surveyed the room for someone willing to take over the discussion. When no one moved, he stepped off the stage and the group again applauded.

"Well, I'm impressed," Stephanie said from the back of the room. She rose and approached his table. "You all did a great job," she praised them. "That's exactly where you have to start when designing an intervention to help move your organization into a new employment agreement.

"And what great lists! Before we move on to answer Bert's question — Where *do* you go with this? — does any one else want to share what your group came up with about the new relationship?"

Stephanie assumed the Chiefs were somewhat intimidated by the work that Bert's table had done. What transpired were a few general comments about the need to be committed to continuous learning, a need to address portable benefits, and the concern that many older workers needed time to adjust to a work environment that was more 'situational' than lifelong. After the Chiefs had made their comments, Stephanie again directed their attention to the work Bert's table had presented.

"Let's start by reviewing the employer wish list." Using the laser pointer, she highlighted the first item. "'Self-motivated employees.' This is not really all that new, is it?" she asked. "Haven't companies always wanted their employees to be self-motivated? In most cases, the answer is yes. But now it's becoming essential for each employee to be capable of self-motivation and self-management. As organizations become flatter, more and more employees will be responsible for these things — after all, there are fewer supervisors now. The employees may find they are working in locations remote from where their boss is located. In fact, weeks or maybe months may go by without the manager or supervisor being visible. From what I've heard you share," she added, "most of your employees already are scattered around the galaxy and not directly under day-to-day observation. "

At the back of the room, the woman who yesterday had identified herself simply as 'Linda' stood. Her full name was Linda Brown and she was Chief of Stunning Stars, a company that helped organizations find qualified workers galaxywide for a variety of clients, especially those in high-tech industries.

"As I'm listening to this, I have a two-part question," she said. "First, what are the employees supposed to do if they're already in an organization and have not cultivated a self-starter mentality? And second, how can organizations be sure that the employees they are hiring are practiced self-starters?"

Stephanie considered this. "Well," she began, "in response to your first question, I think that you can start by letting your employees know that they will be held accountable for their own work performance and career development. Design measurements for success that are linked to your goals, and to their performance review and compensation plan. Let them take it from there. Remind them that acquiring and strengthening work skills is critical, and explain why — again, it relates to their future employability. They need to see that staying abreast of the skills required for their profession will help them distinguish themselves from others.

"Now don't get me wrong. They probably won't be able to do all that by themselves. You may need to help by providing basic training for employees in organizational skills, time management, career management, stress management, communications and/or interpersonal skills.

"Second," she went on, "it is important that the value you hold for self-management and excellent performance be incorporated in recruiting and hiring strategies. You can do that by informing all potential candidates about organization values, providing rewards and encouragement for self-motivation and self-management, and clearly defining measurements for performance. As you're interviewing candidates, I've found, asking for a few examples of how they demonstrated these skills and behaviors in the past helps you find the right person for the job.

"Linda, does that help?" she asked. Linda nodded.

Stephanie turned her attention back to the wall screen. "How about this second item, the one about needing risk-takers? What thoughts do you have about this?" As Stephanie waited for a response, she noticed that Pete was smiling at her. Unwilling to be distracted, she ignored him.

"Given what you told us yesterday about Survivor Syndrome," Harry spoke up, "I don't see how we can expect to get risk-takers when one of the symptoms of the illness is that employees avoid taking risks."

Then Pete chimed in. "Yes, we agree. In fact, when you look over the entire list of employer needs, they contradict the disease's symptoms." Casting his boyish grin at Stephanie, he continued, "Stephanie, are you trying to tell us that before we can expect anything from our employees, we need to provide relief from this illness?"

Stephanie was pleased. "Gee. Listening to all of you and the great responses you have come up with, I'm not so sure you really need me anymore," she said. "You've caught on. And yes, Pete, there is a process to dealing with the impacts of downsizing. Before the organization can move on to establish a new relationship, employees must come to grips with the current reality and commit to taking control of their own futures.

"It may be healing in the sense of accepting reality. It may be healing in the sense of getting to know themselves again and being honest with themselves about their strengths, weaknesses, passions and values. It may be healing in the sense of mapping out an action plan for leaving the current situation for an employer that provides a healthier and happier environment. Or it may be healing in the sense of continuing with the current employment situation and mapping out an action plan to be initiated, only if and when, it is necessary. For everyone, the healing will be a little different. As you probably already know, a lot will depend on the individual's perception of the world, her perception of her capabilities, and the degree of optimism in her attitude toward life.

"Looking back at the list Bert's group came up with — yes, if the employer is to realistically nurture the behaviors necessary to achieve the goals of the organization, there must be recovery from Survivor Syndrome. That should be viewed as the first step to be taken," she indicated, as she poured herself a cup of coffee from the carafe.

"Additional steps that we've mentioned include a clear understanding by all employees of their role and responsibilities in the new organization, as well as actions to improve the understanding of what the changing work environment means for each employee. When your employees are ready to move forward, they will want to take the next step by addressing training needed for their future.

"And finally, as each employee is accepting a future different from what she once envisioned, and preparing herself to be productive in the new environment, the culture also must be changed to support a work force of independent thinking and actions, rather than one rooted in dependency on the company.

"And naturally, all employees strongly desire to be treated with respect and dignity. But picture the process as a cycle," she added.

"In this cycle, both management and workers want to move to independence, control of their own destiny, a flexible work environment, and balance with work and family. But they can't make these things happen until they free themselves from the shock, guilt, anger and depression that plagues them. Like I said, the grip of Survivor Syndrome is crippling. The individual can't begin to redefine herself until she is willing to accept that she must change. Something needs to happen to break the cycle of hopelessness."

Stephanie looked out at the Chiefs. "I submit to you that the break can come when the organization adopts a policy of opening up direct, honest and two-way lines of communication."

A rather large gentleman who had not yet spoken raised his hand. Stephanie acknowledged him. Standing up to address the group, he boomed, "My name is Stanley Rogers. A lot of you know me as 'Bud,' which is a nickname that has stuck with me since I first arrived here about 12 years ago. I'm the Chief Director of Virtual Cove Assembly, our governmental agency that provides services and support to our residents" — this, for Stephanie's benefit.

"As with so many others in this room, my agency has had to face hard times and tighten its belt. We continue to offer more services than we did 12 years ago, but our budget does not grow proportionately. Naturally, our costs continue to climb and we are always searching for ways to improve efficiency through technology.

"But what I have to say has to do with this notion of 'open communication.' One of the biggest problems I've been unfortunate enough to observe is that often, my managers are struggling to deal with their own denial and shock about the situation. So they aren't necessarily capable of carrying the message to the troops in an open, honest manner.

"Do you know what I mean?" he asked in his deep baritone. "Has anyone else experienced this problem? I mean, it's great to say that we need open communication, but we need to realize that the folks carrying the message are human, too, with the same emotions and reactions as everyone else. How do we manage that?" Having had his say, Bud sat, crossed his arms and waited for a response.

"I was looking around the room as Bud was speaking," Stephanie proceeded. "I noticed a lot of you agreed with him. Yes, this is a real problem. I too have seen it, back on Earth. Now that you're becoming familiar with Survivor Syndrome, I think you can see why it is so important to begin training your management team early in the game. They need time to process and adjust to the reasons why the company is considering this decision, what they might expect from their own emotions, and what behaviors subordinates might display when the official announcements are made.

"There definitely is a fine line between creating unnecessary panic by addressing something that may never happen, and helping employees prepare for the future. All I can suggest is that once it's pretty clear to senior management that downsizing will occur, education of managers and team leaders expected to initiate the change should begin."

Stephanie realized that it was getting close to the time for a break, but she couldn't resist relating one of her own stories. She moved from the stage to drift among the tables and began. "I know we're getting close to a break, but I have a story to share that might be helpful. We haven't talked much about interventions yet, but back on Earth, at my company, we also wondered when to involve our managers and how much investment to make in the survivors.

"You see, the way we rolled out the downsizing was over a four-year period. So you might be an internal survivor today, and tomorrow you'd find yourself an external survivor looking for a job. Because this was all new to us, we decided to not involve the managers in direct, open discussions about alternatives being investigated relative to our financial and competitive position. I guess we were nervous about how they would react, as well as slightly embarrassed that our past strategies had not been visionary enough to allow us to avoid a traumatic shift in our culture. So of course the managers and employees had a wild rumor mill going. A real example of 'if you don't tell them the information, they'll make it up.'

"We found ourselves spending so much time addressing the rumors, which were 10 times worse that the facts, that by the time the true information was published, no one — including our managers — knew what to believe. They felt betrayed because we hadn't confided in them. Subsequently, they felt that their own credibility with their employees was jeopardized, and that their ability to reach their performance goals had been sabotaged.

"Believe me, we never intended to have this type of impact on the divisions, and we certainly didn't need to add more confusion to an already emotionally charged environment."

Stephanie found herself standing in the doorway between the auditorium and meeting center. "On Earth we have a saying: 'Hindsight is 20/20.' Well, if we had to do it all over again, and knowing what we know now, we would have included our managers, board, executives and management team.

"Why don't we stop here and pick up after a short break? I'd like to conclude our discussion about creating the new relationship before I meet with your employees this afternoon. If it's okay with you, let's reconvene in about 15 minutes. Harry has again arranged for snacks next door."

Stephanie pushed the button on the wall that opened the gateway to the small lobby, from which adjoining meeting rooms (including the temporary "snack room" next door) were accessible. As she watched the Chiefs file through, it occurred to her how funny it will feel to be back on Earth, where the high-tech gadgets she had almost learned to take for granted these past two days were unheard of.

☆ ☆ ☆ ☆

The room was cleared of everyone except Pete. Somehow, she knew he would remain behind, although she wasn't sure how she honestly felt about it. To be sure, she still felt all the same sparks, but why pursue this? She'd be gone in a few hours and they'd never see each other again.

He was the first to speak. "Stephanie? Speaking of honesty in communications, I have a confession. I'm not sure what to do with my feelings about you. I had such a great time last evening getting to know you. I'm energized by your spirit and compassion for people, and I wish we could have more time together to see where this relationship would lead. I heard Harry say you'd be leaving at around four. I just needed to say these things to you before you go.

"I'm not sure what the future will hold for either one of us," he continued. "I know I'd feel really bad if I didn't get a chance to tell you to your beautiful face the confusion I'm feeling. I know this started out as a traumatic experience for you, but for me it has been not only an opportunity to understand and develop some new strategies for my business, but to experience some feelings that I never thought I'd feel again after my wife was killed. Forgive me if I sound like a babbling fool. I just needed to let you know."

Stephanie was stunned. She knew she had felt the chemistry, but there was no way to be sure he was feeling it, too. This was her confirmation, no doubt about it. But how should she respond? What was in her best interest? She wasn't sure how she should leave this. As the questions performed somersaults in her mind, she heard herself speak.

"Here I am, giving a speech about honest communications, and I was too scared to take a chance and tell you how I felt. Maybe it's because I've had a few heartbreaks that have left some scars. Maybe I wasn't ready to trust myself. But now that you've confessed, I have to admit that I too feel the chemistry between us, and I've been delighted by the fantasy of meeting you and connecting as we have."

She gazed at him, a smile playing at the corners of her mouth. "Nor am I sure where this relationship could go. I mean, there is lots of space, and I do mean space, between where you live and where I live. Perhaps we should just be thankful for the chance to have met and touched each others' lives and leave it at that."

Then she leaned forward and kissed him on the cheek. "I'll never forget you, your hospitality and your warmth," she whispered, her lips close to his ear. "No one will ever believe this cyberspace tale, but I'll always know in my heart it was a trip filled with very special feelings."

She backed away from him, holding his gaze and reaching out for his hand. Suddenly, the doors to the auditorium slid apart and Harry entered. "Hope I'm not interrupting anything," he said, grinning sheepishly. "I thought you said 15 minutes?"

Stephanie squeezed Peter's hand before she let it go. "That's right, Harry. And no, you're not interrupting. In fact, I was just going for a cold drink. I'll be right back."

☆ ☆ ☆ ☆

Stephanie absently watched her group file back into the auditorium, unable to let go of the bittersweet feeling that had invaded her. Time had passed so quickly since she first arrived in Virtual Cove, and so much had happened to her since her inauspicious encounter with the harmless Harry. The thought of being home again, safe and secure in her own environment, was very exciting, but that she would inevitably leave these people behind was beginning to be a painful thought. Despite the short period of time in which she had to do it, she had managed to develop more concern and respect for the people she had interacted with than she would have guessed.

Standing up to address the group, Stephanie appeared refreshed and energized, and ready to begin. "As you re-examine where your organization is in implementing strategies that support the downsizing decision, there are a few issues I'd like you to consider," she said. "One is to realize that when building the new employment contract, you have to look at it as a shared vision, requiring the participation of employees, community, shareholders and customers. The other is to realize that it takes inspiration and courage to rebuild the employment relationship — courage and inspiration on the part of both the employee and employer. That begins with the vision and abilities of leadership.

"But it doesn't stop there," she reminded. "The inspiration and courage to face the future as a team must be supported by practical business systems that electrify employees and inspire visions of the future, rather than one that perpetuates fear and paralyzes them."

Moving to her place at the podium, Stephanie continued. "We've talked about many things over the last day and a half. I'd like to close by recounting the interventions you can design to help yourself and your employees prepare for whatever the future holds."

She picked up the computer tablet and wrote:

☆ COMMUNICATION

☆ EMOTIONAL RELEASE

☆ SUPPORT AND ENCOURAGEMENT FOR
    INDEPENDENCE

☆ SYSTEMS AND PRACTICES

As the words surfaced on the wall screen, she replaced the laser tablet and picked up the pointer. Pointing to the first item on the list, she began her explanation. "The more you can communicate about what is going on in the organization — openly, honestly and compassionately — the quicker you can re-establish a climate of trust."

Highlighting the second item, she said, "Allow the opportunity for employees to come together and express their thoughts and emotions about what they are seeing and feeling. Do it in a constructive environment. It's usually best to work in small groups, and always with the objective of developing an action plan that will yield positive next steps. That's the ultimate goal.

"As you can imagine, the first two things I've listed here are somewhat easy to begin working on and can be initiated without much preparation. But when we get to item three" — point; click — "we're talking about a different story. 'Support and encouragement for independence.' With your leadership, the organization needs to find the courage and patience to begin modeling a different behavior, and to expect everyone to practice that behavior. As we've discussed, again and again, the behavior must be one that shifts from dependency on the company to a more self-reliant one. Each individual must take stock of her own personal inventory and determine how she measures up, whether her performance is the best quality she can offer — the best she can be proud of.

"And finally," she concluded, pointing to 'systems and practices,' "you must ensure that your strategies, policies, practices and culture motivate employees to remain independent thinkers, creative problem-solvers and flexible managers of change. Make sure you are really rewarding the performance and behaviors you truly are looking for. Not a short order, is it?" Stephanie asked, smiling out at the audience.

She paused to let them absorb this information. Then she left the platform and descended into the audience. "I know we've covered a lot of ground since yesterday, and I thank you again for your participation and attention. It has been extremely helpful for me to learn more about your experiences, and I can assure you that the stories you've related will prove useful when I return home.

"I hope your experience has been similar," she concluded, prepared to adjourn. "Are there any final comments before we go?"

Several of her newfound friends expressed their gratitude and praised her for a job well done. Stephanie, pink-eared, accepted their accolades.

As the Chiefs were gathering their notes and preparing to leave Harry suddenly stood. "Sit down, everyone," he instructed, shushing conversation and motioning for everyone to stay put. "Please. Please sit. Just for a minute.

The room, sensing no other choice, quieted, and Harry strode to the middle of the room. Then he turned to Stephanie and began.

"Stephanie, I'm so pleased to hear that you're walking away with new information just as we are," he beamed. "We are so thankful that you fell into our town. For the rest of you, I just want you to know that I've been recording these sessions on our meeting tracker and will have the notes available this afternoon. I'll put them out on the network as soon as they are finalized."

With that, the participants again prepared to depart — but not before each stopped to thank Stephanie for her help and wish her a safe journey home.

☆ ☆ ☆ ☆

LESSON SEVEN

Building Personal Independence and Employability

Harry had wasted no time arranging for Stephanie to meet with about 20 employees of the firms represented at her previous sessions. That gave a nice cross mix of organizations. The variety would, in Harry's words, "give you a good inside view of what we're dealing with."

The meeting was to take place at the bank's retreat center on the edge of the community park. Stephanie was to join the group for lunch before initiating discussion. As both Harry and Pete had been involved in the logistics of this meeting, they accompanied her to the center and made the appropriate introductions. Then Harry gave Stephanie a note with instructions that detailed how to reach him when she was finished and ready to return to Earth. He knew he would be in meetings during the afternoon, sharing this new information with his management team, but he was committed to taking a break whenever Stephanie was ready. Anyway, it wouldn't take long to send her on her way.

Harry said good-bye. Pete exchanged meaningful glances with Stephanie, and they smiled. Then they left, leaving Stephanie to ponder a romance that could never be.

When Stephanie and her new group of friends had finished eating, they convened in a conference room set up with small oval tables designed to accommodate four. Although the setting was not as sci-fi as Harry's office, it was still less conservative than anything Stephanie had experienced on Earth. The walls were a muted, textured paper done in cranberry and teal. The lighting was soft and warm - very relaxing.

After everyone found a seat, Stephanie got things rolling. "I appreciate Harry and Pete arranging for us to meet," she began. "As you may have heard, I've spent the last day and a half talking with your managers about the impact the decision to downsize has on survivors. The reason I'm interested in this topic, and I guess I'd have to say somewhat knowledgeable, is that my firm on Earth also has been going through it. We mutually agreed that it would be helpful to share what I knew with your managers, and to explore their experiences and observations. I'm glad that all of you also have agreed to meet with me. I think we have a lot to learn from one another."

123

As Stephanie was only going to meet with this group for a few hours (no more extensions, she told herself) she decided to rely on the technology available in Virtual Cove to assist her with her presentation. She felt it was important to provide some background before she began, much like she had with the Chiefs. So she played some key portions of a CD-type recording that had been produced from the meeting with the Chiefs. Specifically, she queued on discussions about what Survivor Syndrome is, and how it affects the personal health of the individual and the health of the organization. She also queued the definition of an intervention and some descriptions of what an intervention would be.

As the computer was finishing with the programmed topics, Stephanie stood up and asked, "What is your reaction to these definitions? Have you heard these words before? Have any of you been studying the affects of downsizing on organizations?"

A young woman named Sydney was the first to speak. "I'd just like to say that it already has been worth my time to come to this meeting," she said. "I at least now know why I've been feeling the way I have been. I was worrying something was wrong with me because I was so depressed, fearful of making a mistake, untrusting of my boss and even my co-workers. Now I realize that those are normal feelings for the situation I'm dealing with. Thanks."

Stephanie acknowledged the young woman's appreciation with a smile and a nod. The ice having been broken, another group member — this time a man — stood up to speak.

"My name is David. And I work at Virtual Travel. It used to be a swell place to work, but now the morale is so low. There is no energy or excitement and employees, including myself, are more apt to communicate into the main scheduler our inability to make it to work for situations that, in the past, we never would use as an excuse. I'm glad to hear you talk about teaching us interventions, or ways to modify our behavior so that we can make the best of our lives again. I really think that is everyone's goal. No one wants to get up in the morning and make plans to have a miserable day."

As David took his seat, the group laughed with him, entirely familiar with the routine of planning the day from hell.

"As we only have a few hours together, I'd like to use our time to help you understand how to build personal independence. In doing so, I think it will be helpful for us to begin by talking about what it's like to be in an organization that's going through all these changes. Sometimes, when you're not necessarily in a position that helps to shape policies, chances are you feel helpless.

"I'm curious about what your issues are and if they are similar to those of the employees on Earth with whom I've spoken. I also wonder if you are finding it necessary to let go of your dependency on your organization and learn how to rely on your own capabilities to manage your careers?"

Stephanie didn't have to wait long for someone in the group to instigate discussion — it was one of the women she had observed in Harry's cafeteria. "My name is Mildred," she offered timidly. "For me, the hardest thing to deal with is not knowing when my job might be eliminated. I hate to spend time planning to manage change in my future if my job is never going to be cut.

"But on the other hand, I struggle with why I'm waiting. Yes, no job is really secure anymore. I know that. But I want to do a good job for my company and be considered for future positions. I'm not sure if others here have the same concern, but I'd be interested in talking about it." As Mildred sat down, Stephanie made a mental note of the body language in the room. Mildred was not alone, she decided.

"Well, Mildred, thank you for getting us started. I think the concern you have raised is a common one. One thing I hear time and time again is this struggle of *when* and *if* to begin planning for the future. I personally believe the battle is rooted in the fear of giving yourself permission to shift your paradigm about the firm from one of a maternal relationship to one based on economics. It's hard to give up the 'family' image of the firm and realize that from now on, your job is as secure as the economic situation dictates.

"The first step is to realize and accept that the company has made a business decision to downsize. The center of your energy should not focus on whether that was the right or wrong decision, or whether it is good or bad for the company. Your energy must be focused on the reality that this is what's happening, right now, and you must prepare yourself to be flexible, open to change and less resistant to stepping outside your comfort zone in order to make the most of the changed work environment. Now is the time to plan for the day when you might need or want to do something different, either inside or outside your current company. Take charge of your destiny, beginning now."

Stephanie looked around the room, struck by the utter lack of energy. They were emotionally bankrupt, or appeared to be. Demoralized spirits. It struck Stephanie as sad. Unfortunately, she had seen it before.

126

"I know what I'm suggesting is not easy to do," she suggested, kindly. "I know all of this is very painful. But if you want to be a player in the future with your company, you need to prepare yourself to get in the game. Don't just watch from the sidelines. Now don't get me wrong. There is no guarantee for a job. But as things change you'll be better prepared with a positive attitude and updated skills."

A young man stood up and identified himself as Ken. He had been with the Cyberspace Bank for about 10 years.

"What you're saying seems pretty abstract," he said. "I guess I need to know which steps to follow if I'm to arrive at this state of independence. Do you have any models that we might follow as we try to give ourselves permission to change?"

Stephanie picked up a computer tablet similar to the one she had used in Harry's auditorium. "I think we can make one up," she replied. As she began to write, the window over-looking the park disappeared beneath a screen that unfurled to reflect her comments.

"First, I'd say you have to accept reality for what it is and implement an action plan to stop any behavior or thoughts that describe you as a 'victim.' That means stop looking for some-one to blame for this disruption and stop complaining about the changes being implemented. Take positive action to feel better about what is happening, and educate yourself about what you need to take care of yourself.

"Now remember: You're not becoming independent so you can quit your job. Your purpose in becoming independent is to realize your employability within your current organiza-tion, or in others at which your talents and skills are required.

"Maybe we should step back and define the term inde-pendent. 'Independent' means being free of influence and control of the maternal organization. Think of it this way. If you're in a spaceship, flying around in outer space, wouldn't you feel better being the navigator, instead of flying blindly with the controls in the hands of someone else?"

Many of the participants acknowledged her comments with a nod. She could see others struggling with the idea of letting go of dependency on their company. From her experi-ence on Earth, she knew how hard it is to take full responsi-bility for one's own actions and future.

"Well, that's what I'm suggesting," she continued. You chart your own course. Don't wait for the organization to tell you what move you need to make next."

Stephanie queued the computer to play the segment of the previous session that dealt with the history of employment relationships on Earth. It was essential to provide insight into why the organizations had developed the control and influence she was now suggesting they move away from, she decided. After all, what she was suggesting they do was inconsistent with what traditionally had been a maternal-child relationship. She knew she couldn't just waltz in and tell them to make drastic life changes without providing a substantial base for her proposal.

She saw a hand go up at the front of the room. She acknowledged the woman, who introduced herself as Angela, and requested that she stand up to make sure her comments could be heard by everyone. Angela obliged.

"Stephanie? I've been able to follow everything you said so far," she began. "But you lost me when you got to the part about getting in touch with what's 'right for me.' Maybe I'm wrong, but it sounds like you don't think we know what's best for us. I'm puzzled. Is that what you meant?"

"That's very perceptive of you, Angela. Yes, I am suggesting you need to take stock. But I don't mean to sound like you're not capable of knowing what's best. Based on my experience, I'd be willing to assume that all of you are suffering from some degree of dependency on your organization. I really don't see how you *can't* be. Like I said, organizations in the past were built on purposes, missions and strategies to tie you into depending on them for almost everything.

"For example, how many of you have made a career-changing decision without the company first coming to you and advising you that you were ready to take on new responsibilities? How many of you have the core of your social interactions linked to people or activities at work? Or how many of you rely on your organization to keep you informed of the latest in technology in your field, instead of reading, learning and networking with others outside your company for a different perspective?

"Can you see where I'm headed? The nature of the past culture put employees in a very dependent position.

"So I'm just suggesting you get comfortable with the fact that you need to get rid of some level of dependency and become more independent. For each of you, the degree of dependency probably differs. But the bottom line is all the same: You need to shift your paradigm.

"One of the side effects of dependency is that individuals learn to suppress what they value and believe in order to please someone else. Namely, your boss. Because you've been disciplining yourself to please your boss and give up your own ideas and values, you need to spend some quality time getting in touch with what you've buried. Ask yourselves what's important to you."

Stephanie continued to stroll the room. "I'll share a comment with you that someone in my office said to me. This came from a woman who had been with our firm for 12 years. She was just beginning to reconnect with what was important to her, where her passions were. Very early in this journey she commented that, for the last six years, she had been doing the job of computer programmer because that's where the company said it needed her. It wasn't until she was reconnecting with her values that she realized this wasn't even the type of work she liked to do. She eventually transferred to our accounting department and is much happier.

"That was quite an eye-opener for her, to realize that what she might want to focus on might have nothing to do with her current responsibilities.

"Now, once again, I'm not suggesting that you get comfortable with change and develop a plan so you'll leave the organization. The idea is to be employable — not just employed.

"Think of this as a great opportunity to revisit what is important in your life and, if necessary, make some changes. We have a saying on Earth, that every cloud has a silver lining. Yes, the impacts of downsizing are painful. But there is another side of the process that is limited in its possibilities only by the limits you choose to put on yourself. I hope something we talk about here today will contribute to your success in developing your independence, so you can learn how to awaken your passion, joy and commitment. Then you can put them to work for you in your professional and personal lives.

130

"Just think about how much happier you would be about your job if you had the same spirit and excitement you had when you first started with the company. Didn't that make a difference in how you did your job?"

Taking a break to pour a glass of the ruby-colored fruit drink offered on the refreshment table, Stephanie continued, "I don't know if you're familiar with trends we're seeing in the workplace, but certainly we're moving to a more mobile, flexible work force. Of course, every organization will always have some type of core full-time permanent workers, but supplementing that core will be workers who are part-time, and others who are on contract for a specific period of time and for a specific task. Be mindful that a similar type of arrangement may be in your future, which makes developing independence even more important."

The next to offer his observations was a fellow by the name of Don, who worked in Rita's organization. As he spoke, the frustration in his voice was unmistakable. "Stephanie, I'm not doubting that you have many cases upon which to base your comments. But I keep getting hung up on what this new relationship is like without the loyalty and dedication employees had in the past. How will organizations be successful without it?"

Without warning, Angela jumped from her chair. Facing Don, her voice brimming with anger, she retorted, "Even if they came back and said they were sorry for what happened in the past, for the decisions they made and for the way they treated employees who were leaving and those of us who stayed — even with all that, I couldn't trust them again. There is no way I could ever be loyal and dedicated like I used to be. There is no way I would sacrifice my health and my family time like I did for so many years. I'm ready to put myself first, because if I don't think about myself, no one will." She plopped back into her seat, and was rewarded for her outburst with enthusiastic applause.

"Don, I'd have to say that my experience supports Angela's remarks," Stephanie agreed. "I've seen more individuals tuning into a new radio station than ever before and the station is WII.FM— What's In It For Me. I believe most employees feel so violated by the way things are handled, it would be difficult, if not impossible, for them to recover their previous commitment and loyalty. But on the other hand, I believe they do want to find common ground with their employers, and work in an environment of mutual respect and dignity.

"But all is not lost. Employers and employees who recognize this new mindset can build the new relationship by addressing both needs. They can develop partnerships around training, job rotation and special assignments as a way to augment the employee's skill base. In turn, the employee should continue to do an outstanding job for the organization. There still is something being traded, but the relationship is adult-adult rather than parent-child. Each partner is determining whether the exchange is for something of value, and if they feel it is a fair exchange for what they're giving.

"Does that help you paint a different picture of how this new relationship might look?" Don nodded, but Stephanie wondered if it was premature to expect him to see it.

She continued. "I'd like to point out that the organization also receives many benefits from supporting the movement of employees to independence. It's not all stacked in favor of the individual." Turning to the screen, Stephanie's words appeared:

☆ INDEPENDENT WORKERS FOCUS MORE ON THEIR PASSION FOR THEIR WORK

☆ INDEPENDENT WORKERS ARE LESS AFFECTED BY SURVIVOR SYNDROME

☆ IT'S EASIER TO ENABLE INDEPENDENT WORKERS TO TAKE CHARGE

☆ TEAMS ARE MORE PRODUCTIVE WITH INDEPENDENT WORKERS

☆ COMMUNICATION FLOWS MORE FREELY AMONG INDEPENDENT WORKERS NOT PARALYZED BY FEAR

☆ PERFORMANCE IS MAXIMIZED (INDEPENDENT WORKERS ARE MORE CONSISTENT WITH QUALITY)

Don again raised his hand. "Let's say we embrace this notion of independence. What responsibilities do we have as workers to make this happen, and what should the organization do to support it? In my firm, we don't have eye contact, much less meetings to keep us informed. The grapevine is busy and that's where most of our information comes from."

"I'd like to share an observation with you that is identical to one I shared with your Chiefs," Stephanie replied. "We could be having this conversation on Earth, and all of you could be in my company. Reactions to the loss that comes with downsizing is universal, no matter what solar system you're in.

So: How do you do your thing and what should the organization be doing? Well, let's talk about you first. I can't stress enough the need for you to get comfortable with continuous learning. I don't mean just seminars offered in cyberspace. I mean, use every available minute to expose yourself to new information that will keep you on the leading edge of your profession. You've got so many learning opportunities here in Virtual Cove — use all that technology has to offer, and then, add old-fashioned methods such as listening to motivational tapes, reading trade journals, and getting involved with networking with others in your industry, inside and outside of your company.

"I also think it is important that you spend some quality time developing your personal mission and goals. Put them in writing, too. What have you done so far with your life and what else is important for you to achieve?

"Once these goals are written down, develop a step-by-step action plan of how you'll get there. Keep in mind that you have the luxury of still having a job while you're doing this work. That should allow you a little more time for exploration and self-discovery. But don't let that be your crutch," she warned, "or you won't ever begin. Be glad you still have the job. But prepare yourself for a future of continuous change.

"As you make your journey to independence, assess your skills and expertise. Ask others for honest feedback on your strengths and weaknesses. Look for ways to reconnect with work that is stimulating and challenging, and aligns with your real interests and passions. Rekindle the things that are of value to you in the world. And as you think about the things that must change in your future, don't forget the things you value and want to hold on to. This time around, hold onto to your identify and values and don't sacrifice them unless you're aware that you're doing so and that it's okay with you."

The room was very still.

Stephanie was very aware that she must treat this group with compassion and empathy. Their expressions and body language belied their depression and hopelessness. She now saw why Harry and Pete had mentioned poor morale and reduction in productivity. These folks were emotionally exhausted.

"So often, employees in my organization tell me they're only staying for the paycheck and the benefits. I certainly can appreciate that in our society, which is based on economics and a monetary system, a paycheck is important. But why wait until things are different and no money is coming in for several months? Be proactive and be prepared. Give yourself permission to face the future with confidence knowing who you are and what good work you do.

The room wasn't just still, Stephanie decided. I can hear some of them breathing.

She continued. "My last suggestion for you to think about when building your plan to achieve personal independence is to practice an intervention that should be very eye-opening to you. Does anyone remember what I said an intervention was?

A woman named Zena raised her hand and Stephanie invited her to stand. "You told us it was an action taken to modify a behavior that was negative or destructive," Zena replied with a smile, and returned to her seat.

"That's exactly correct, Zena. Thank you. Now let's take

some time to work with one right now. But you should make at least an hour available to revisit this when you have some quiet time to reflect on the questions.

"This intervention has three parts. First, I want you to write down the things that you perceive as barriers in becoming independent — the things that are holding you back from being freer. Take a few moments to write down what immediately comes to your mind."

As she gave them time to write, Stephanie walked around the room. She knew she couldn't ask them to share what they were writing — it was too personal. But she was curious to see if what they listed would be similar to the barriers expressed by her employees in Atlanta. She was not disappointed as she saw:

I can't get this kind of salary anywhere else

I need all the benefits for my family, especially the free virtual travel

I'm too afraid of starting all over in another company. Even if I don't like this one, I at least know what to expect

Who would want someone at my age

Fear of EVERYTHING!

135

After sufficient time had passed, Stephanie continued. "Okay, on a second page, list all the things you value. These are things you don't want to lose as you plan for the future." After giving them a few moments to collect their thoughts, Stephanie asked the group to call out their values as she scribed the list that magically transferred to the wall screen:

☆ HONESTY

☆ INTEGRITY

☆ CREATIVITY

☆ FRIENDSHIP

☆ QUALITY

☆ COMMITMENT TO GOOD WORK

☆ LOVE FOR MYSELF AND FAMILY

Looking up at the screen, Stephanie asked the group for a reaction to what they saw. She was pleased when they realized others in the room also held dear those values.

"The last part of this intervention is for you to develop a third list — your action plan for ridding yourself of the barriers on the first list even as you hold on to the values stated on your second list. Begin with a small-step approach to remove each barrier from your path. For example, if benefits and wages are critical for you, if you must have them without interruption, perhaps you could investigate alternatives to coverage in case you lose your job. Establish a savings account to cover the cost of the benefits and several months of wages. If you look hard enough, you will discover a workable solution for most of these barriers, whether they're real or perceived. Trust me, I've tried this and have used it in my organization many times, and the results are surprising.

"Now let's go back to Don's question. How is the organization responsible for assisting with the shift to a more independent work force, and for nurturing it so that it stays that way?

"The first thing I'd say is, it has to start at the very top. The Chiefs of your organizations must be willing to commit to a change and, for that matter, model the behaviors they expect from all their employees. They must reward workers for taking the risk to be independent. They must ensure that policies, procedures and strategies support this type of environment, and that funds are earmarked to develop and train workers to embrace this change."

A young woman stood and introduced herself: Cindy, from Stunning Stars. "I've heard a little about what you've been telling our managers," she said. "My Chief, Linda Brown, stopped by the office last evening after your session and shared some of what you've talked about, and I have a question. Is this why you've been talking to them about opening up communication? I can see that if we had more open communication, we'd need less direction from our supervisors about what behaviors are expected to fulfill our vision and mission. We could just focus on getting our tasks done. Is that right?"

Stephanie was so pleased. She loved it when the light bulb clicked and ideas revealed themselves to be linked by a coherent pattern. "That's exactly what I was talking about, Cindy. If you know up front what is expected, you can funnel your energy directly into your work, rather than waste it attempting to second-guess why you were asked to do something.

"Speaking of communications, another responsibility of the company is to identify and eliminate inappropriate management styles for dealing with independent workers," she went on. "The management style of the future must focus more on *coaching* individuals, not directing their every move. It must include the skills for giving and receiving feedback, and coaching workers through problem-solving, rather than just providing the answer. The 'control' mentality is what got companies into this dependence mode in the first place. We have to give that up.

"I have two final comments about the organization's role in all of this. One is that employees should be rewarded when their behaviors align with what the company wants. The other is that employees might need help managing an effective balance between work and family. Times are changing. Organizations have to be more flexible if their employees are to embrace change and independence. Concrete examples of providing flexibility include telecommuting, flex-time schedules, daycare options, time-off policies, a sabbatical program and so on."

Stephanie stopped to sip juice from her glass, and a man in the back stood to address the group. "My name is Gus. I know almost everyone in this room. — I've been in Virtual Cove for about 14 years now. Anyway, the one thing I'd like to see us spend some time discussing is the effect all this change has on survivors' stress levels. I don't know about everyone else, but in my business I'd say our stress level has gone way up, because of all the work that remains after the staff is cut. What about the rest of you?"

Everyone agreed.

"That's a problem in my company, as well," Stephanie commented. "Thanks for bringing that up, Gus. It's important for each individual to assess where she is with stress and to choose how to appropriately deal with it.

"Let's make a list of how you all are currently handling it. Who's going to start?"

One by one, suggestions appeared on the screen:

MANAGING STRESS

EXERCISE

JOURNAL-WRITING

MEDITATION AND YOGA

HOT BUBBLE BATHS

SUPPORT GROUP OR COUNSELING

STRESS-MANAGEMENT TRAINING

PLAYING SPORTS

PLAYING A MUSICAL INSTRUMENT

HIKING AND ENJOYING NATURE

BREATHING EXERCISES

WORST-CASE SCENARIOS

STAR GAZING

TIME OFF TO DO NOTHING

VACATION

When the list had accumulated, Stephanie turned to the group. "Well, you are all quite busy. I'm pleased to see you have so many ideas for ways to control stress. As you consider stress, remember that different levels of stress require different actions. The most proactive thing you can do is to take a periodic measure of your stress level and then, if necessary, choose the appropriate action to get it back under control."

Stephanie looked at her watch and realized that her time with the group had almost expired. "I'd like to share one more vision with you. Take this as a snapshot of what an independent worker might look like," she said, moving to the small podium where her notes had been stationed. "Relax in your seats, close your eyes and try to picture yourself with these characteristics."

In a soft, calming voice, she read, "The independent worker is loyal to her needs, while she allows the quality of her work to determine her employability. She gains power from making her own choices and supports her team members to achieve their stated goal. As an individual committed to independence, she thrives on continuous learning and self-exploration, and is energized by her self-confidence and self-affirmation. Using this energy, she continually seeks to strengthen known weaknesses, takes charge of herself and motivates her own actions. As an ethical and valued member of the universe, community and company, she practices honest, open communications and defines herself by who she is, not where she works. She recognizes her work is never-ending, as she continues to feed the courage to step outside her comfort zone.

"I hope you all were able to imagine that profile fitting yourself. It's a great goal to have.

"I wish I had more time to spend with you and explore more of these survivor issues," Stephanie said, as if in apology. "I hope I have given you some ideas that you will spend some time exploring. My wish is that all of you will find the courage, enthusiasm and passion to begin building your bridge to tomorrow. I do believe it will help you find happiness, not only in your professional careers but in your personal lives.

"Thank you," she concluded, feeling herself blushing. "Are there any quick last-minute questions I can answer before I go?"

Elaine, an older woman who had been visibly absorbed in the session, raised her hand and stood as Stephanie began to straighten her notes. "Before you go, Stephanie, I was wondering if you could suggest some articles, books, lessons or whatever we could look at to help us with this process?"

140

"That's a good suggestion, Elaine. I have a list already prepared that I share with my employees back on Earth. Is there anyone here that can help me get into my computer files in Atlanta so I could pull the file for you?" Stephanie was amazed to hear herself making such as outrageous suggestions to link computers between Virtual Cove and Atlanta. It's time to get back to reality, she told herself.

That's when Joe from 21st Software jumped up and said he'd be glad to show her how. "No sweat," he informed her.

The group applauded indicating their appreciation of Joe's efforts. (Refer to the final section - Recommended Readings.) As the group left the room, Stephanie smiled content with herself for making the time available to meet with them. She knew it was just as important as spending time with the Chiefs.

But now it was time to go.

☆ ☆ ☆ ☆

PART THREE

THE RETURN

Per Harry's instructions, she met him in the park on the bench where they had first exchanged names and stories. As Stephanie waited for him to appear, she reflected on all that had transpired. Nothing ever changes, she thought, and people don't really connect and communicate until they personally touch.

If she hadn't taken Harry's hand when he had extended it, what would have been the outcome? If she hadn't listened with empathy as he talked about his work situation, she would have missed out on a lot. And if she hadn't taken the risk to get to know Pete, she would have missed making a very special new friend. Maybe that was what this was all about: finding ways to connect with other human beings, one person at a time, and making the connection with respect, dignity and the recognition that not everyone is the same.

As she saw the pieces of this two-day puzzle form more clearly from the fuzzy edges of her mind, she became aware that Harry was standing in front of her.

"Ready?"

"Yes. Harry, thanks for everything. I'll never forget this place." She then rose from the bench and stood next to him.

As she stood, Harry took her hand. "Nor will we forget what you have shared," he replied. "Have a nice trip"

Stephanie straightened up, startled to find herself in front of her computer. Her elbows were numb, as though they had rested in one spot for too long. She glanced quickly down at her clothing, surprised to see that she was wearing the same faded bluejeans and T-shirt she had put on that morning, and her mind swelled a little with panic. What happened to those wild clothes she had selected from the computer catalog?

She rubbed her eyes (hazy either from sleep or from gazing into cyberspace) and glanced around her, hoping to find some evidence of what she had been up to for the past two days. Finding none, she slumped in her seat and breathed a heavy sigh.

No way.

It appeared as if she had just nodded off for a cat nap. It was still raining and the clock on her computer read one. One p.m.? Or a.m.? She quickly checked the computer's calendar for the date and stared in disbelief when it read Saturday instead of Sunday.

She was totally disoriented. Had she just been dreaming, or had she really been to Virtual Cove? Were Harry and Pete and Rita and all the other Chiefs just a dream? Even if they were, it was a sad thing. She would miss them.

144

And anyway, how would she begin to explain to her friends what had happened?

She decided to get up, make a cup of tea and put the idea of Virtual Cove away. Clearly, she had been dreaming. There was nothing to suggest otherwise.

☆ ☆ ☆ ☆

Stephanie sat at the table, happily munching an egg salad on rye. She hadn't realized until now how famished she was. She sorted through the mail on the table as she ate; was disappointed only to find bills and junk mail. Finishing her lunch, she decided to return to the computer. She would go back to square one, and try once again to stay awake and enhance her knowledge of the Internet.

Hastily brushing the crumbs from her T-shirt, one cheek bulging from the last bite of sandwich, she headed for the office. Before she could focus and reconnect to the Internet, she had to note some ideas about new interventions and approaches she wanted to try at work on Monday. She wasn't sure where the thoughts were coming from, but she knew it would be useless to try to concentrate on anything else until she wrote them down, lest they be forgotten.

"Initiate feedback on what survivors want to help them prepare for the future," she wrote. Suddenly her eye caught something flashing in the corner of her computer screen. It was the icon that notified her of the arrival of e-mail messages.

She opened the file. Startled, she read:

Stephanie, I hope to see you soon. I miss you.

-Pete.

PART FOUR

HARRY'S NOTES

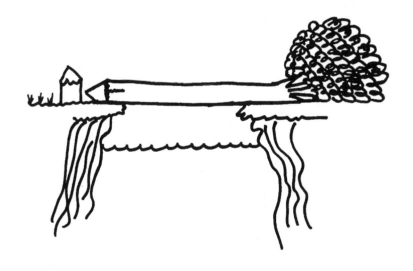

LESSON ONE

Survivor Syndrome: A Sickness that Affects the 4 Ps: Profitability, Productivity, Performance and Personal Health

Survivor Syndrome is a term used to describe the attitudes, beliefs and behaviors of employees who remain with an organization after a downsizing. The syndrome does not discriminate based on length of employment — all employees who remain with the organization after the downsizing is announced are survivors. They may survive another day, a week, a month or several years. The fact that the culture and expectations of the organization are changing is what activates the virus.

All individuals, including managers, should be aware of what Survivor Syndrome is. Survivor Syndrome can be paralyzing to employees. To recover, the employee must understand what is happening to him or her and then begin the process of arriving at accepting the reality of the situation. This is accomplished by taking stock of current behavior and planning the appropriate steps to modify any negative, destructive or nonproductive behavior exhibited. It's also important to assess how the syndrome is affecting performance and relationships with co-workers and customers. The employee and employer are both better served when the employee has initiated these actions to move from a dependent relationship to one of independence and self-management.

149

Survivor Syndrome is rooted in the psychological contract. This contract is defined as an implied relationship between the employer and employee with the "understanding" that, if the employee did a good job, was loyal, dedicated and willing to make sacrifices for the company, the company would reciprocate by taking care of him/her until retirement or resignation.

Implementing such drastic business strategies as downsizing challenges this (implied) arrangement and erodes employees' confidence in the organization. They feel violated and abused.

Employees suffering from Survivor Syndrome exhibit such behaviors as narrow-mindedness, aversion to risk, confusion about their role in the new organization, distrust of management, inability to effectively focus on team goals, preoccupation with job instability, and even random acts of violence (at work or home) and sabotage. This type of behavior impairs the organization's ability to achieve its performance and profitability goals — indeed, the company is hindered by weakened productivity, lack of commitment and dependability, lower quality of work, low morale, greater absenteeism, and higher costs associated with any employee assistance programs implemented. In addition, the personal health of employees is affected as a result of greater stress, erosion of confidence and esteem, and anxiety about future unknowns.

150

Employers must address the needs of both employees being asked to leave and employees who are staying. Research indicates both share similar feelings and emotions about the changes they are experiencing.

LESSON TWO

Integrating the Needs of Business, Employees and Community

The Integrated Downsizing Approach (IDA) is a model that can assist organizations in the development of a win-win downsizing strategy. The purpose of the model is to clarify the three stand-alone plans that work in concert to address the various elements of preparation, implementation and follow-up.

The three stand-alone plans include the downsizing plan, dismissal plan and survivor plan, but a core group of identical components thread through each. This model addresses the needs of the business, the employees and the community; all three plans function as a three-legged stool, of sorts, that must be implemented in a balanced and integrated manner. One plan out of sync with the others will cause the stool to tip over.

During the development of the **downsizing plan**, the team has the opportunity to explore alternatives to the one designed to permanently lay off employees. Measures such as early retirement, attrition and job-sharing with competitors should be investigated. If downsizing still is determined to be the appropriate response, the development of this plan will define the scope of the downsizing, clarify why this action has been taken, and determine specifics about how the plan will be communicated.

In determining the scope of the downsizing plan, the organization may want to investigate plans other companies have employed and incorporate any lessons learned (that is, whatever the company is willing to share). The team working on this plan also will need to consider the condition of current employee relations, the training necessary to prepare managers to carry out the plan, and the financial impact of all proposed recommendations.

The **dismissal plan** includes the type of severance package or outplacement support that will be offered to employees being asked to leave. This plan also outlines what process will determine who will be asked to leave. The process should be documented, easy to understand, fair and equitable, and — without question — consistently practiced.

It also is critical to recognize the company's citizenship position while developing and implementing this plan. Not only are employees watching the company as it plans for and communicates this process, but customers, stockholders and the community at large also will judge whether the approach is humane. Companies often assist departing employees with support for emotional stress, training to update job-search skills and networking opportunities.

The third plan focuses on defining the **new employment contract** in alignment with the organization's new vision and mission. The team will be identifying which polices and procedures will be updated to mirror the roles and expectations of the new culture. Performance measurements, compensation strategies, and reward and recognition programs all will need to be revisited and brought in line to reflect the new behaviors and accountability expected of each employee.

This plan must address emotional elements similar to those included in the dismissal plan. Employees remaining with the organization need an opportunity to express their feelings and emotions about the changes occurring in the company. They also need assistance with transitioning to the new culture and adapting to the future employment relationship, which will be structured as a self-managed career rather than a lifelong one. This assistance might include resume preparation, and interviewing and networking skills.

All three plans are linked by similarities that must be incorporated into each. The common elements include perception of the organization's citizenship role; the opportunity to grieve; nurturing employees so they enable themselves to face the future; encouragement and commitment to continuous learning; obvious commitment to the new employment relationship; recognizing that individuals have different capacities for change; a reasonable pace for implementing changes; realistic cost estimates and time frames for action; generation of buy-in and commitment; frequent communications; and updated procedures (as necessary).

LESSON THREE

Coaching Yourself and Others

In order to help other employees manage change, managers — from the top down — must first heal themselves. Therefore, training and support should be offered to those managers involved in implementing the downsizing strategy before it is rolled out to the rest of the organization.

It's important that each employee gets in touch with and expresses her feelings and observations about what is happening. Remember, if people are denied that opportunity, their emotions eventually will be exposed through behavior. Until employees have a chance to let these emotions go, they will continue to focus their energy away from productive work and concentrate on a futile effort to find the source of their pain.

153

Managers should realize the importance of strengthening their coaching and feedback skills. As employees become more independent and less reliant on the organization for an assessment of performance, values, definition of quality of work and social structure, the employee will be less receptive to a management style that directs and "tells." The metamorphosed employee will be receptive only to a management structure that treats employees as adults, mentors rather than directs their development and, where appropriate, uses a team approach to coach the work process so that every member's contribution is valued.

The manager must not take on the responsibility of solving each employee's problems. Instead, the manager should initiate a dialogue of open-ended and probing questions that assist the employee with the process of self-discovery. That's why the interpersonal skills of the manager should be continually strengthened. It is these skills that are more and more in demand as a component of a successful organization.

LESSON FOUR

What's Driving Downsizing Strategy

More than 9 million U.S.-based workers lost their jobs, permanently, between 1991 and 1993. As of June 1996, there was a 28 percent increase in jobs lost over the same period in 1995.

It does not appear that this strategy is waning. To the contrary, it appears more and more as if it is a management prerogative. A survey conducted in 1995 polled U.S.-based companies that had implemented major restructuring, and found that most believed their companies were more efficient and competitive **before** the restructuring and downsizing.

154

So why do companies still decide to travel this road? There are many reasons, any one of which (or a combination of several) could act as a catalyst. Common culprits include competition, advanced technology, lack of awareness of what competing companies are doing, mergers and acquisitions, excessive costs, lower demand for products and services, the absence of structural flexibility that would allow quick response, excessive bureaucracy, sporadic work volume and globalization.

Executives should heed lessons learned by companies that have gone before them. One such lesson might involve out-of-balance workloads created by downsizing without restructuring the work process. The impact is the same amount of work for fewer employees, thereby creating potential confusion and potential problems with quality and customer service. Another lesson is the impact the implementation process has on internal survivors. If the process is handled poorly and employees believe they are not being treated fairly, or if they perceive they are not being treated with dignity and respect, the resulting behavior may manifest itself as a statistic that indicates 156 million work days are lost every year to depression.

There also is a price to be paid for the loss of loyalty from the work force. Fifty-three percent of the workers in downsized organizations report the mood at work is angrier than in previous years. Executives should be aware that internal survivors suffer from stress, burnout, anxiety, anger, insecurity and cynicism.

LESSON FIVE

Minimizing the Effects of Negative Emotions and Behaviors

Understanding emotions associated with Survivor Syndrome is important. But to minimize the effects of these emotions and behaviors, it's necessary to develop effective interventions for oneself or for one's work team.

To put things in perspective, compare the emotions an individual experiences when faced with the possibility of losing a job to those attached to the loss of a loved one. The emotions are parallel, from denial and depression to anxiety and anger, guilt and, finally, hope and acceptance.

Realize, too, that travel through these emotions is nonlinear and subject to change at any moment.

It is extremely important to legitimize whatever emotion the employee expresses. This can be a difficult task, especially for a co-worker or manager who has not experienced that emotion. Remember: They are where they say they are. What's more, not all work groups will travel through the emotions together, or at the same pace. It is a very personal journey.

Avoidance, shock, denial and disbelief characterize the first phase of the grieving model. Because it is known that employees generally will respond with these reactions, it is essential to demonstrate and model the behaviors that the company is looking for. The managers need to "walk the walk" and "talk the talk." Failure to do so will reinforce for the employee the notion that nothing is really changing; in that case, it isn't fair to expect them to do anything but hold themselves in denial and ignore the changes the company actually is trying to implement.

An extreme sense of violation may surface in the second phase, which is confrontation. (Indeed, that violence in the workplace has increased over the past few years is attributable to this feeling of having been wronged.) The confrontation period is underscored by the employee feeling abused by the company — after all, in her mind, the psychological contract has been broken. The employee may demonstrate behavior that stems from anger and guilt. That's why security issues should always be a part of any downsizing plan, as should providing assistance for the employee to work through her anger. Take proactive steps to diffuse the situation.

Expect anger, expect mistrust and expect that it will take time for employees to accept what is happening, understand the changes and react in a positive manner. Helping employees through this process will help expedite the time it takes for the organization to get down to the business of focusing on the future.

Gradually, employees will relinquish denial and begin to accept the reality of the situation. This phase is called re-establishment. At this point, the employee may not agree with the decisions the company has made, but she at least is willing to accept that the employment relationship has changed — and that she is expected to take more responsibility for her performance and career management.

There are many avenues by which individuals will arrive at this point, but all of them will require some degree of personal discovery and reflection. The employee will need to re-examine her personal and professional skills, abilities and experiences to determine where she wants to focus energy for the future. This particular task is enlightening, for it should help her uncover what it is she feels passionate about.

Taking this journey further means the individual will make decisions about what kind of continuous learning to pursue, to stay current with job expertise and aware of leading-edge technology and required skills. Personal education goals should be established to help the employee realize her 'passion,' whether it be harbored within her current work function or elsewhere.

157

In other words, this is every employee's chance to take control of her destiny. By doing so, she will move further from the employer-dependent relationship and gravitate toward a new model of the work relationship, which is more personally driven, more economically centered and situational (that is, determined by project needs, not lifelong).

LESSON SIX

Benefiting from the Changing Employment Relationship

The old employment relationship was rooted in loyalty, dedication and commitment, which developed in part because employees wanted to secure their jobs, financial futures and benefits coverage. Inevitably, this practice evolved into a dependency relationship and an expectation of entitlement.

But things have changed. With current circumstances surrounding downsizing, employees are filled with fear, mistrust of management and anger toward the company. Many employees hold little hope for the future before realizing they hold the power for their future in their hands. Naturally, these emotions make it difficult to find the right balance for the new employment relationship.

It is possible for employee and employer to benefit from a new employment contract. However, the employer who initiates changing the employment rules must realize that employees will now be more concerned about pleasing themselves than pleasing the employer. That's why the employer must understand what the employee wants, and decide whether it's reasonably achievable (or even if it can be done) under the new business mission. (Certainly, in either case, all employees will appreciate this type of open, honest communication.)

The process of recreating an employment relationship will be expedited if the organization sends a clear, firm message of the vision and mission of the company, along with the commitment to collaborate on a new relationship. This can be done by incorporating competencies deemed valuable into hiring and recruiting strategies, as well as performance appraisals and recognition programs. To underscore that commitment, continuous learning opportunities should be offered that will support 'employability' rather than just employment.

Companies should want valued employees to stay, but it's important that they stay for the right reason — that is, they have decided that this is the company, the job, and the task that links with their passions and career interests.

The new employment relationship can be viewed as a circle, in which employees make the effort to collect the skills to be independent. They then use that independence to take control of their destiny, remain resilient to continuous change, and be flexible in order to maintain balance between work and family. Abetting this cycle are interventions afforded by open, two-way communication; assistance with gaining skills to manage change; preparing managers to implement these organizational changes; support of training to maintain the most current (i.e., useful) employee skills; and benchmarking policies that reflect the new culture in terms of compensation, hiring, performance management and rewards.

As a result, the organization meets and may exceed its performance and profitability goals, and the cycle continues in an upward spiral — taking the company and its re-energized employees to new heights.

159

LESSON SEVEN
Building Personal Independence and Employability

(Compliments of Stephanie)

It is difficult for the still-employed to accept that they must begin building a bridge to tomorrow. It's difficult because their current state of being employed precludes a sense of urgency. Frequently, they avoid investing time in preparing for the future because they've convinced themselves, possibly from a place of denial, that they may not lose their job after all. So why take any action?

Whatever can be done to (in a positive way) encourage the employee to prepare for the future, and whatever can be done to support employees in that preparation, will be beneficial to all.

Each employee must get comfortable with what needs to be done. She needs to understand that she is not engaging in these preparations in order to quit her job; rather, she's doing so because there's always the possibility of moving to another job — either within or outside of the current organization. This process will require that she consider the influence the maternal organization has had on her before she can cut the strings and stand on her own.

To be sure, this process requires courage and patience on the part of both employer and employee. The first thing is getting the employee to realize she suffers from some degree of dependency on the organization. However, the focus should not be on the degree of dependency, but rather on which interventions will help guide her toward independence.

It may help the employee to write down the things she perceives to be holding her back. After the list is made, it will be easier to develop a small-step approach to overcome any barriers noted. In this exercise, it is important for the employee to determine what is really of value to her. This information, as well as self-discovery exercises, will prove invaluable as the employee works through the changes in the work environment and begins pinpointing opportunities that reflect her personal values and interests.

It takes courage, time and commitment, but as employee and employer build a bridge to the future, each benefits. The employee is becoming more independent in overcoming Survivor Syndrome, resulting in significant behavioral and performance improvements that benefit the organization. As the threat of Survivor Syndrome diminishes, and both parties redefine the relationship into one built on mutual respect and dignity, the organization will be better-situated to achieve production, performance and profitability goals.

GLOSSARY

Benchmarking The quantitative measurement and comparison of an organization's business processes against competitors and other organizations with similar processes.

Change Management The techniques used to create and sustain changes within an organization.

Downsizing The planned elimination of jobs resulting from a combination of potential threats and a belief that the organization structure is overgrown with excess jobs.

External Survivor A person who is no longer employed by a company after an involuntary employee reduction. External survivors must start over in jobs that may be similar to, or quite different than, what they had been doing.

Internal Survivor An employee who remains in an organization after an involuntary employee reduction. Internal survivors are faced with moving the organization into the future.

Intervention A powerful act designed to modify behavior deemed nonproductive, negative or personally destructive.

New Employment Relationship A relationship created to replace the psychological contract, based on mutual respect and dignity for the needs and goals of the employee, the employer, and the stockholders and customers.

Organizational Citizenship An internal standard of correct behavior by which the organization demonstrates sensitivity to ethics, fairness and equity when dealing with individuals, methods and systems.

Psychological Contract An unwritten, implied agreement between employers and employees, in which employees who perform and fit into the organization's culture expect the employer to employ them until retirement or until the employee decides to leave.

Survivor Syndrome A term that describes a set of attitudes, feelings and perceptions that typically occur in internal survivors.

RECOMMENDED READINGS

Boroson, W. & Burgess, L. (1992). "Survivors' Syndrome," *Across The Board*, November 1992, pp. 41-45.

Cascio, W. (1993). Downsizing: "What Do We Know? What Have We Learned?" *Academy of Management Executives*, Vol. 7, No. 1, 1993, pp. 95-104.

Conner, D. (1993). *Managing At the Speed of Change*. New York: Villard Books.

Harrington, W. (1996). "Reduction in Force: When the Ax Fell at USGS," *The Washington Post Magazine*, May 19, 1996, pp. 15-32.

King, D. (1996). "Seeking the Cure for Ailing Corporations," *Organization Development Journal*, Vol. 14, No. 1, 1996, pp. 5-22.

Isabella, L. (1989). "Downsizing: Survivors' Assessments," *Business Horizons*, May/June 1989, pp. 35-41.

Labib, N. & Applebaum, S. (1994). "Strategic Downsizing: A Human Resources Perspective," *Human Resource Planning*, Vol. 16, No. 4, 1994, pp. 69-92.

Maes, J., Rushing, D., and King, D. (1996). "Some Lessons Learned From U.S. Workforce Reduction," *Equal Opportunities International*, Vol. 15, No. 4, 1996, pp. 10-13.

Noer, D. (1993). *Healing The Wounds*. San Francisco: Jossey-Bass Publishers.

The New York Times Company, (1996). *The Downsizing of America*. New York Times Books.

Westberg, G. (1992). *Good Grief*. Fortress Press.

ORDER FORM

SHIP TO:

Name_____

Street Address _____

City_____ State_____ Zip _____

Phone_____ Fax _____

E-mail Address_____

QUANTITY	UNIT COST	AMOUNT
_____	$17.95	_____

SHIPPING & HANDLING
First Book $5, add $2 for each additional book   _____

SALES TAX - GEORGIA RESIDENTS
All Georgia residents add appropriate sales tax   _____

TOTAL   _____

SEND ORDER FORM WITH CHECK MADE PAYABLE TO:

EMI Publishing
1700 Little Willeo Road
Marietta, Georgia 30068.1734
770.587.9032
evolumgt@ix.netcom.com

*If for any reason you are not completely satisfied you may return
the book for a full refund.*

ORDER FORM

SHIP TO:

Name_____

Street Address _____

City_____ State_____ Zip _____

Phone_____ Fax _____

E-mail Address_____

QUANTITY	UNIT COST	AMOUNT
_____	$17.95	_____

SHIPPING & HANDLING
First Book $5, add $2 for each additional book   _____

SALES TAX - GEORGIA RESIDENTS
All Georgia residents add appropriate sales tax   _____

TOTAL   _____

SEND ORDER FORM WITH CHECK MADE PAYABLE TO:

EMI Publishing

1700 Little Willeo Road

Marietta, Georgia 30068.1734

770.587.9032

evolumgt@ix.netcom.com

If for any reason you are not completely satisfied you may return the book for a full refund.